Faith
in Doubt

SIMON P. WOODMAN

Text Copyright © 2023 Simon P. Woodman

Illustrations Copyright © 2023 Dawn Savidge

Independently published by Swanzy Publishing, 2023

All rights reserved.

ISBN: 9798356817380

DEDICATION

This book is dedicated to the congregation
of Bloomsbury Central Baptist Church,
who have laughed, cried, prayed, and praised
their way through the last decade with me.
I am grateful to be their Minister.

CONTENTS

Dear reader 1
Words of gathering 3
Words of approaching 13
Words about money 39
Words for the world 43
Words inspired by scriptural texts 85
Words for the Lord's table 121
Words for times and seasons 137
Words of blessing 187
Words of doubt and faith 193

ACKNOWLEDGMENTS

Thank you to Revd Dawn Savidge for the illustrations and artwork. Dawn has ministered at Bloomsbury alongside me for many years, and was present when many of these prayers and poems first saw the light of day.

I am thankful to those who have helped me in the preparation of this book, especially Revd Dr Karen Smith whose constructively critical voice I have long valued.

Finally, and once again, I am grateful to Liz, for everything.

DEAR READER

Thank you for picking up this book of words, which I pray will speak of the possibilities of hope and faith. I believe very much that words matter, whether spoken, thought, or written; and that the words we use in church matter very much, because they are public words, and such words shape worlds. To speak them is to invite people to inhabit the worlds we have glimpsed and long to inhabit.

Some eschew the written word for the extempore utterance, relying on the inspiration of the Spirit in the moment of congregational engagement. Occasionally this has been my experience too. But more often I have preferred to trust the inspiration of the study over that of the pulpit; and this means that I script most of my sermons and many of my prayers.

After a decade of ministry at Bloomsbury Central Baptist Church, and as I entered my sixth decade of life, I found that I had enough prayers written for public worship, across a variety of liturgical contexts, to consider sharing them more widely. And so this collection was conceived: an anthology of prayers presented so that others might reuse them, adapt them, and find inspiration in them; with some poems and short stories to provoke and invite further reflection.

I pray these words are a blessing to those who read them, and that they shape a more loving, more hopeful world for us all to live in.

Simon Woodman, Bloomsbury Central Baptist Church.

WORDS OF GATHERING

To believe, and even more to assert publicly, that we are gathering into the presence of God, is no small thing. To start with, it sets out what we believe about who *we* are, and who we believe God to be.

At Bloomsbury, our practice has often been to gather using a responsive pattern, as the people and leader call each other into worship. This interplay of call-and-response creates an expectation that in the service that follows, there will be a dialogue between those who speak from the front, and those who respond from the pews.

There is something that is expected of each of us, as we gather to respond to God. On our best days, we come with expectancy and hope, listening to everything God might be saying to us. Some days we come distracted and unfocussed. But always we come longing to hear God speaking to us in worship, and longing to respond to God. Our whole act of worship is therefore 'responsive', inasmuch as it expects a response from all who have taken part in it.

For gathering in love, faith and hope

May the Creator of love give us new hope.
We are a people of hope.

May the Son of hope give us new faith.
We are a people of faith.

May the Spirit of faith give us new love.
We are a people of love.

So we come to worship in love, faith and hope,
We are God's people.

For gathering to meet God and be changed

God of love and joy and hope,
we gather to meet with you.

God of forgiveness and new life,
we gather to be changed by you.

God of each moment of our lives,
we gather to offer ourselves to you.

For gathering in the certainty of God's presence

God is always with us, and never deserts us;
We bring our praise to God today.

God is always within us, present to each moment of our lives;
We open our hearts to the Spirit of God.

Christ is always beside us, whatever our difficulties,
We turn to Christ in trust and faith.

We are the people of Christ, sustained by his loving Spirit.
We are Christ's people, and we offer ourselves to his service.

For gathering to turn towards Christ

The Lord Jesus calls us into his presence,
we come to meet him by his Spirit.

The Lord Jesus calls us to repentance,
we turn away from our sins and towards him.

The Lord Jesus calls us to new life,
we lift our eyes to the future that is set before us.

We gather to worship the Lord,
he has called us and we have heard him.

For gathering as the family of God

God of love, you call us to be your family,
and we rejoice that you love us.

God of unity, you call us to live in harmony,
and we commit ourselves to the path of peace.

God of hope, you call us to face the future with courage,
and we trust ourselves to your loving care.

God of each moment, you call us to have faith,
and we offer ourselves to your service.

For gathering in the certainty of God's presence

God is with us in all things,
God is with us today.

God is with us in the wilderness of confusion,
God is with us today.

God is with us in the safe and secure places,
God is with us today.

God is with us, even when God cannot be seen,
God is with us today.

God is with us when we know God's presence,
God is with us today.

God is with us in Jesus Christ,
God is with us today.

For gathering in need of new life

God of new life,
we offer to you our whole lives.

God of wholeness,
we offer to you our brokenness.

God of healing,
we offer to you our infirmity.

God of restoration,
we offer to you our disconnectedness.

God of wholeness, healing, and restoration,
we receive your gift of new life.

For gathering in the name of Jesus

Lord Jesus, Lord of life, Lord of hope,
we gather in your name.
We hear your call on our lives.

Lord Jesus, bringer of comfort, giver of peace,
we gather in your name.
We hear your call on our lives.

Lord Jesus, healer of our wounded souls,
we gather in your name.
We hear your call on our lives.

Lord Jesus, creator of new life,
we gather in your name.
We hear your call on our lives.

For gathering to worship God revealed in Jesus

God who is the centre of all things,
We worship you.

God who is revealed to us in Jesus Christ,
We worship you.

God who is made known to us by the Spirit of Christ,
We worship you.

God who draws all the world into your loving embrace,
We worship you. Amen.

For gathering in equality

Inspired by Psalm 49

Let all people hear the wisdom of God:
All are equal in the sight of God.

Let the wise and the foolish hear God's wisdom:
All are equal in the sight of God.

Let the rich and the poor hear God's wisdom:
All are equal in the sight of God.

God's love extends to all, for all eternity:
Our lives find their meaning in the love of God.

For gathering in light, life, and love

Inspired by John 1

Lord of endless love, you call us into your presence:
In you we find light and life.

Lord of eternal light, you come to us today:
In you we find life and love.

Lord of everlasting life, you welcome us today:
In you we find our eternal home.

For calling people to the journey of faith

From slavery to freedom, from darkness into light.
Out of Egypt you have called your people.
From despair and depression to wholeness and hope.
Out of Egypt you have called your people.

From compliance and complicity to subversion and resistance.
Out of Egypt you have called your people.
From hesitation and distrust to exploration and adventure.
Out of Egypt you have called your people.

From stagnation and apathy to journey and pilgrimage.
Out of Egypt you have called your people.
Through wasteland and wilderness, through hardship and sadness.
Out of Egypt you have called your people.

You call us to journey through desert and Jordan.
Out of Egypt you have called your people.
With sacraments of water and manna to keep us.
Out of Egypt you have called your people.

Through Miriam and Moses, through prophets and pastors.
Out of Egypt you have called your people.
To fulfil the promise of Canaan and Kingdom.
Out of Egypt you have called your people.

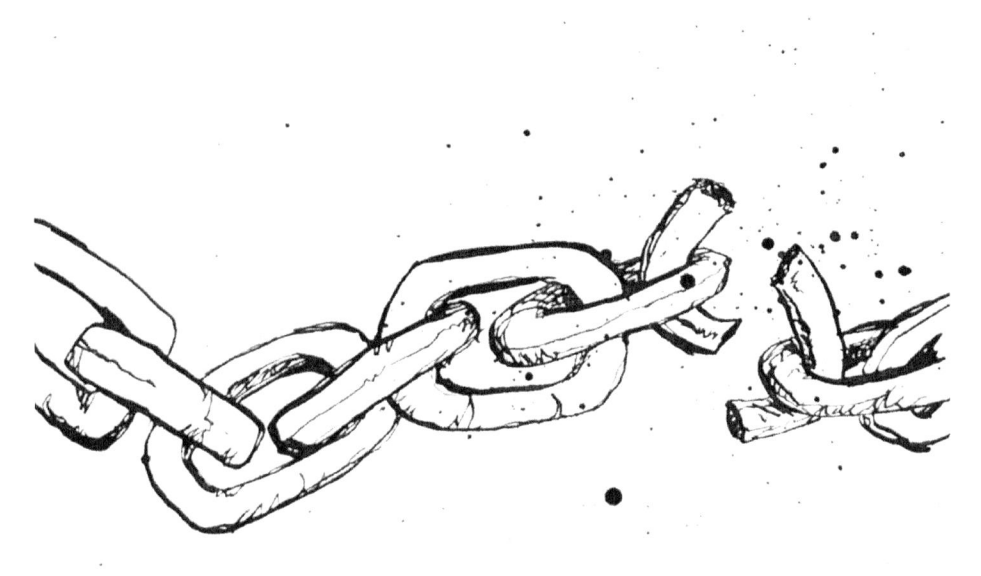

For gathering in troubled times

Inspired by Psalm 46

The world changes, our certainties are shaken, yet
God is our refuge and strength, a very present help in trouble.

Nature turns against people, and people turn against nature, yet
God is our refuge and strength, a very present help in trouble.

The nations are in uproar, and society totters on the brink, yet
God is our refuge and strength, a very present help in trouble.

God is with us, the God of Jacob is our refuge.
God is our refuge and strength, a very present help in trouble.

God says, 'Be still and know that I am God'.
**God is our refuge and strength,
we turn to God in these troubling times.**

For gathering in Advent: Wise Men come

We journey along well-known paths:
We come to worship Jesus.

We journey along ways lesser travelled:
We come to worship Jesus.

We journey through trails and danger:
We come to worship Jesus.

We journey with only the Spirit to guide us:
We come to worship Jesus.

From diverse lands, by routes unknown:
We come to worship Jesus.
We come to worship Christ, the new-born king.

For gathering in Advent: longing for salvation

God of Advent,
we long for the day of salvation,
and we trust in you.
The Lord is our righteousness.

God of Advent,
we long for justice and mercy in our land and our world,
and we trust in you.
The Lord is our righteousness.

God of Advent,
we long for the coming of your promised one,
and we trust in you.
The Lord is our righteousness.

God of Advent,
we long for you to heal the world with love and mercy,
and we trust in you.
The Lord is our righteousness.

For gathering on Mothering Sunday

God of love, mother of us all,
we give thanks for the life that you have brought to birth in us.
Loving God, thank you for your tender care.

God of love, mother of us all,
we give thanks for your steadfast love for each of us, your children.
Loving God, thank you for your tender care.

God of love, mother of us all,
we give thanks that you sustain us and support us throughout our lives.
Loving God, thank you for your tender care.

God of love, mother of us all,
we give thanks for the church which nourishes us, and enables us to grow.
Loving God, thank you for your tender care.

God of love, mother of us all,
we give thanks for the gift of those who love us, and those whom we love.
Loving God, thank you for your tender care.

WORDS OF APPROACHING

I envisage the opening prayer as a continuation of our words of gathering, albeit often separated in practice by an opening hymn: we have already called one another to worship, and now we dedicate ourselves as individuals and as a community to the task of approaching God in worship.

As we do so, we often bring our confession and hear words of forgiveness.

The opening prayer is often followed by saying together the words of the Lord's Prayer, and at Bloomsbury we use a version that is in contemporary language and which avoids using gendered language for God:

Loving God in heaven, hallowed be your name,
    your kingdom come,
    your will be done on earth as in heaven.
Give us today our daily bread.
Forgive us our sins
    as we forgive those who sin against us.
Lead us not into temptation,
    but deliver us from evil.
For the kingdom, the power and the glory are yours
    now and forever.
Amen.

For a renewed vision of God's faithfulness

Faithful God, we give you thanks and praise
    that you never abandon us, that you never desert us.
May we never forget your steadfast love for us,
    may we never forget your mercy shown to us.

We trust that you are merciful and gracious,
    slow to anger and abounding in steadfast love,
and we thank you that your love for us
    stretches to the heavens and down to the depths.

We thank you that you release us from our sins,
    and that you have compassion on us all.

As we gather here in worship today,
    may we catch a renewed vision of your faithfulness
        to all that you have made,
and may we be granted once again a renewed strength of purpose
    to live as *your* people,
bringing life to the hungry and hope to those in despair,
    release to those in captivity and good news to all who live in fear.

Amen.

For entering the presence of God

God of love, you invite us today to enter into your presence.
    You invite us to come as we are,
        to bring with us all our joys and sorrows,
        all our successes and failures,
        all our worries and concerns.

You invite us to reflect in your presence on the stuff of our lives,
    and to receive from you words of love, words of assurance,
    words of forgiveness, words of transformation.

We are truly sorry for those times
    when we have been less than you would have us be,
for when we have hurt others and ourselves
    by our thoughts, words, and deeds.

So we come, loving God, trusting that you will receive us.
    We come, trusting that you will never turn away from us.
    We come, trusting that our lives can be redeemed by your love.

God of love, you come to us in Christ Jesus,
    reaching out to us wherever we are, whoever we are.

God of love, you come to us by your Holy Spirit,
    entering into the depths of our souls
    to bring your love to the ground of our being.

So, God of love, we come,
    and we are met, and we are transformed.
For this we offer our thanks,
    and we join together in the words of the prayer
    that Jesus taught his disciples…

FAITH IN DOUBT

For courage, wisdom and truth

Great God of all love,
> we offer ourselves today to your service;
> and we lay our whole lives before you.

Great Spirit of all wisdom,
> we offer our minds to your service,
> and our souls to your scrutiny.

Give us the courage to loosen our grasp on the truths we hold dear,
> as we open ours hearts to the larger and deeper truths
> that you have yet to reveal.

Forgive us when we prize our own certainties
> over humble trust in your eternal wisdom.

May we know you in the renewing of our minds,
> and in the refreshing of our souls.

May wisdom and truth take us by the hand,
> and lead us in discovering new paths of peace.

And so we pray together the prayer which Jesus taught his disciples…

For lives that are complex

Loving God, sustainer of all that exists
        and origin of all that shall be,
we gather in the name of your son Jesus Christ
        to offer ourselves once again to your service.

We come into your presence with strength and weakness,
        with hope and despair,
        with love and with hate,
        with joy and with sorrow;
and in all the complexities of our lives
        we trust that you will meet with us,
        redeem us, and transform us.

So we ask your forgiveness for those times and places
        where we have betrayed your calling,
where we have treated others and ourselves
        in ways that deny your love for everything and everyone
        that you have called into existence.

Renew us today by your Spirit,
        for works of service to your coming kingdom.

Heal the brokenness of our souls,
        strengthen the weakness of our spirits,
        and restore us to be the people that you want us to be.

Free us from our enslavements and addictions to other gods,
        and teach us the true freedom in life
        that we find through our dedication and devotion
            to your path of love, peace, and righteousness.

And so we pray the prayer that Jesus taught his disciples…

For gathering to be transformed by the Spirit

Lord Jesus, son of God, we gather today in your name;
        and as we gather, we offer ourselves for transformation
        by the influence of your Spirit moving amongst us.

May we hear your words anew,
        and gain a fresh sense of their power in our lives.

May we be open to the gentle whispers of your Spirit,
        as you challenge our preconceptions,
        comfort our anxieties,
        and absolve our failings.

May we worship with honesty,
        and pray with integrity.

In humility we acknowledge our sins,
        and we recognize that we have done things
            that should have remained undone,
        and that we have not done things
            that we should have done.

Forgive us, and reassure us of your ongoing love
        that surpasses all our attempts to betray it.

We pray now for all those who will serve us in worship today,
        and we thank you for readers and singers,
            for preachers and pray-ers,
        for musicians and stewards,
        for those who offer gifts practical,
            and for those who offer gifts spiritual.

We pray for one another.

And we join our voices together
        as we pray the prayer that Jesus taught his disciples…

For gathering as the children of God

God who is like Father and Mother to us all,
> giver of all love, all hope, and all joy,
we gather in your name to be shaped as your people.

We come to this time of worship as individuals,
> from many circumstances and diverse contexts;
but we come longing to find you in the midst of our gathering,
> and to discover you as we encounter one another.

So keep us attentive to those around us,
> help us to hear your voice in the voice of the other,
> and to see you in the face of our neighbour.

Forgive us for those times we have neglected your call on our lives,
> and remind us that you long to draw us back
> into your loving embrace of welcome and acceptance.

So we pray that our time of worship today
> will be a time of holy discovery,
as we learn more of you,
> and discover what it means to be your children.

Amen.

For gathering in gratitude

God of light and life,
  we come to you today in gratitude
    for the gift of this new day, for the gift of one another,
  and for the gift of your great love
    shown to us through your son Jesus Christ.

Help us as we gather in your name
  to discover you in the singing,
  to hear you in the preaching,
  and to encounter you in one another.

We ask for forgiveness
  for those times when we have ignored your call,
  and shut our eyes to your presence in our lives and in our world.

We recognise that too often
  we only see and hear our own voices and activities,
  and that we become too focussed on ourselves.

Lift our eyes and open our ears, and show us more your love.

Amen.

For gathering in praise

God of all creation, we gather in your name to offer you our praise.

We know that there is nowhere we can go to flee from your presence,
        because you are in and through all things,
            and all that exists is sustained by your loving command.

Help us to learn to rest in your presence,
        to find our security in the assurance of your love,
and to discover our true selves
        as we learn to see ourselves and one another as you see us.

Forgive us for those times where we try to hide ourselves from you,
        when our thoughts, behaviours, and habits take us away from you.
Bring us back into your loving embrace as you forgive us our sins,
        and renew us for your service.

Amen.

For entrusting our lives to God

Loving God, we come to you in confidence that you will forgive us,
        but asking that you will help us to forgive ourselves.

May we know the freedom of being wrong sometimes,
        and the joy of not having to always be right.

Lead us forwards into our uncertain future
        with confidence that you love us,
and gift us the creativity and courage
        to explore new possibilities before you.

Amen.

For gathering in weakness

God of glory, God of humility;
> God of might, God of meekness;
>> God of power, God of gentleness;
we draw near to you today in worship,
> conscious of the contradictions that lie at the heart of our lives.

May we discover, through our encounter with you today,
> that you meet us in the midst
> of the mess and muddle of our lives.

Where we are weak, give us strength.
> Where we are self-reliant, teach us humility.

Where we are broken, bring us to wholeness.
> Where we are arrogant, make us kind.

Where we are sinful, bring us forgiveness.
> Where we are in denial of our sin, bring us to honesty.

In all things may we know your presence,
> through the Spirit of your son our saviour Jesus Christ.

Amen.

For gathering in the presence of others

Lord Jesus, our friend and our brother,
> we have come to worship today to meet with you.
May we discover you in each other,
> may we see your face in the face of our neighbour,
> and may others find you in us.

Draw alongside us, we pray,
> in ways that inspire us to live better lives.
Teach us to focus on the needs of others,
> and to be sensitive to those who are hurting.

Forgive us for those times
> when we have not behaved as you would like us to,
and help us to forgive others
> when they have behaved badly towards us.

Show us what it is to live together as members of your family,
> and give us the gift of love for one another.

Amen.

For gathering in community

God of each moment; God of our past, present and future;
    we give thanks that you are with us today.

However it is that we have arrived at this place;
    whatever the circumstances that surround us,
    whatever the emotions we bring with us;
we rejoice that you are present in our midst,
    welcoming us with open arms and loving acceptance.

Help us to discover you in one another,
    help us to hear your voice in the words of the service,
    help us to encounter you in the worship we offer.

Forgive us for those times when we deny your presence;
    when we think and act in ways
    that distort your love, and reject your welcome.

Teach us to live in love, to worship with integrity,
    and to listen with honesty.

Amen.

For gathering to be renewed in worship

God of all good gifts, giver of life, and sustainer of hope,
    we offer ourselves to your service today.

Help us to draw near to you in our worship,
    and may we receive from you
        the renewing of our minds and souls
    that comes from a fresh encounter with your creative Spirit.

May our hearts be attuned
    to your whispered words of love and acceptance.

Forgive us for those times when, through thought, word, or deed,
    we deny your love for all that has been made, including ourselves.

May our harrowed lives be receptive to the fresh seeds of your kingdom,
    and may we bear the good fruit
    of love, joy, peace,
        patience, kindness, generosity,
    faithfulness, gentleness, and self-control.

Amen.

For gathering in trust and unity

Loving God of all people and all places,
    we come before you today as your children,
    scattered yet gathered.

We trust that you are uniting us with one another
    even as we are united with you through your son Jesus Christ.
We pray that your love which enfolds us will hold us
    - individually and communally - this day and in the days to come.

We confess our fear and our uncertainty,
    and we ask forgiveness for our sins.
Renew us and restore us, give us the gift of hope,
    and the assurance of your eternal love.

Amen.

For gathering in difficult times

God of the tough times and the good times,
    God of sorrow and joy, tears and laughter;
we hold before you the trials of today;
    we pray for those whom we love
    and for those who we are called to love.

May our lives display the truth of our faith,
    and may we know the peace of Christ
    that reaches into the turmoil of our lives
    to bring comfort and hope.

Amen.

For dedicating today to God

God of love and light and laughter and love,
    we offer today to you, with all of its joys and sorrows.

May we learn to meet you in the midst of our ordinary days,
    and to find places that allow us
    to encounter your peace and your joy.

Amen.

For inclusion in church life

Lord Jesus, you died for all people.

Forgive us for the ways
    in which we have sought to remake your body after our image.

Show us instead how we can be remade in yours.

May we not exclude those who are not like us,
    and may we learn to see your likeness in all people.

Amen.

For a Church Anniversary

Inspiring God, our living, loving, creative creator,
        we worship you,
and we bring before you today
        our hopes and aspirations for our life together.

On this Anniversary Sunday,
        we give thanks for all that has gone before
and we give thanks for all those who have gone before.

And so today, as we gather in your name,
        to hear once again the stories of faith,
and to encounter the risen Christ
        by the power of the Spirit,
we ask for a renewed vision for our community of faith.

May we receive anew a vision for the church
        which embodies the values of the kingdom of God.

May we be a church where power is held lightly
        and money is released from the tyranny of control.

May we be a church which exposes the oppressive politics
        which masquerade as normal and universal truths.

May we be a church where the good news of Jesus Christ for all people
        is made real amongst us.

May we be a church where all are welcome.
        May we be a church which manifests unity through diversity.

May we be a church where our weaknesses are completed in you,
        as we find strength together.

May we be a church where the kingdom of heaven
        breaks in upon us,
        and is made real amongst us.

As we commit ourselves once again to this vision
        we pray the prayer that Jesus taught his disciples…

For a baptismal service

God of new beginnings,
> we gather in worship today before an open pool,
and we hear once again the echo of your command
> to go into all the world,
to make disciples of all nations,
> and to baptise in the name of the triune God.

We rejoice with …, and we stand with them,
> as they enter into a life of obedience to your call.

We offer our thanksgiving
> for all those who have stood alongside us over the years,
reminding us of your love when we have doubted,
> and offering us support when we have stumbled.

Forgive us for those times when we could, and should,
> have done things differently,
and renew us today to serve you with our whole hearts,
> with our purified minds, and with all of our strength.

Amen.

For Good Friday

God of death and life,
> God who dies and lives,
we gather today in the shadow of death,
> to hold before you the mystery of our lives.

We remember those whom we love, who have died;
> and we remember that we too will one day face death.

Here at the foot of your cross,
> we bring our confession for our sins,
trusting that because of your cross,
> the power of evil has no eternal power over us;
and that in you, we are released from our guilt and shame,
> as we lay our burdens before you.

May we meet you this day in the vulnerability of life,
> and in the tragedy of death.
May we be united with you in mortality,
> even as you draw us into life immortal.

Amen.

For Palm Sunday

Lord Jesus, our King, we welcome you into our midst;
        and we rejoice that you enter
                the gates of our lives, and our community,
        not with force to coerce or control,
                but with love to liberate and renew.

Forgive us when we turn away
        from your gospel of good news for all people,
        and try to proclaim your kingdom after our own desires.
Teach us to listen to you,
        to hear your words of grace and forgiveness,
        and to put what we hear into action in our lives.

Break through the barriers we erect around our hearts,
        and may we encounter you in humility and honesty.
We rejoice that you have come to us, that you are with us,
        and that you will be with us always.

Amen.

For Mothering Sunday

Great God of all love, we come into your presence today
        as people in need of your loving embrace.

We recognize that our independence of spirit,
        and our desire to make our own way in the world,
        have sometimes taken us far from you;
and we acknowledge the many ways
        that we have pushed you away.

We are sorry for those times when we have turned our faces
        away from your loving gaze.

So today, trusting in your unconditional acceptance,
        we open our lives to the light of your love;
and we ask that you will forgive us those dark places
        in our souls and in our lives
            where we have tried to keep you out, and ourselves hidden.

Help us today to hear you calling us once again,
        speaking words of love, forgiveness, and acceptance.

Amen.

Lord's Prayer for Mothering Sunday

God of all love, divine mother of us all,
> your name is holy to us.

May your loving embrace enfold our lives and our world.

You sustain us every day of our lives,
> from birth to death.

You do not turn your face away from us,
> and you enable us to not turn away from others.

Inspire us to live lives of love,
> but keep us safe from those who enact hatred.

For your loving embrace is eternal, unbreakable, and unconditional;
> today, as it always has been, and always shall be.

Amen.

For Harvest Sunday Communion

God of creative abundance,
>we give thanks this harvest Sunday
>for all that is good in our world.

For sunshine and showers,
>for warmth and for cold,
for plants and animals,
>for food and for drink,
>for bread and for wine.

We gather in the name of your son,
>to offer our gratitude for the tangible blessings of our lives.

We thank you especially for the food we shall eat today,
>and for the people who have prepared it for us.

We thank you for farmers, and pickers, and packers,
>for transport infrastructure, for drivers and pilots,
for all those who get our food to us day by day,
>and for those who will prepare it for us to eat.

As we share bread and wine together today,
>may we be reminded of your love for all that you have made.

Help us to be mindful of the diversity of creation,
>and teach us to act in ways that respect your image,
>as it is present to us through all that you have brought into being.

Forgive us when we act in ways that abuse the planet,
>and help us to discover ways of living that are at ease with nature.

Forgive us our sins, and give us today our daily bread.

Amen.

For Remembrance Sunday

Great God of all peoples and all places,
    we come into your presence today
    to remember all those who have died in war,
and to commit ourselves once again to the path of peace.

Sometimes, the weight of the world's suffering
    is too heavy for us to bear,
and we struggle to give voice to the longings of our hearts.

Sometimes, silence before you is the only way we can speak.

So quiet our hearts,
    and speak to us, your words of peace and justice.

May our conflicted souls find reconciliation before you,
    and may we become those who bring healing to others
    and to the world around us.

We stand in the shadow of the cross,
    remembering that violence and death
    lie at the heart of the human experience.

But we live in the light of the resurrection;
    and dare to believe there breaks a yet more glorious day,
as your in-breaking kingdom of peace
    turns tears of sadness to tears of joy.

For this kingdom we long and live.

Amen.

For waiting in Advent

Loving God of Advent, we await your coming.

We gather in your name today,
    in expectation of encounter with you,
but we know that there is nothing we can do
    to hasten your presence among us.

And so we wait for you.

And as we wait, we open our hearts and minds
    to the scrutiny of your Spirit.

Show us those places in our lives
    where we have closed the door to your presence;
convict us of our sins and selfish actions,
    that we might be forgiven and transformed
    by your coming into our midst.

Come, Lord Jesus.
    Come in power, come in weakness,
    come in judgment, come in forgiveness,
    come in our joy, and in our sorrow.

Come to your people,
    that we might discover your presence
    and know the love that you kindle in our cold hearts.

Come to us that we might become
    the agents of your in-breaking kingdom
    of justice and peace.

Come, Lord Jesus.

Amen.

For creative openness in Advent

Inspired by the wise men taking another path from Herod in Matthew 2.12

Surprising God of unexpected endings,
    we enter your presence with lives half-lived.

And we bring with us the gifts of
    our hopes, our dreams,
        our expectations, and our fears.

We bring the years that have passed,
    and the times still to come.

And in this moment, we ask that you will meet us
    through the restless Spirit of your eternal son,
    our saviour Jesus Christ.

Come to us in time, and show us the path to eternity.

Forgive us for those days we depart from your way,
    and lead us ever back to you
        as we travel roads as-yet unknown.

Give us creative minds and open hearts,
    that we might be sensitive to the stirrings of your Spirit,
as you bring order from chaos, peace from conflict,
    love from hate, and hope from despair.

Surprising God of unexpected endings,
    in whom all of eternity finds its meaning,
we offer you our lives and our world,
    and we trust you with all that lies before us.

Amen.

For Christmas morning

Lord Jesus, we greet you this morning,
       as we gather to celebrate your birth.

Lord Jesus, we greet you this day,
       as we gather in your name,.

Lord Jesus, we see in you the hope of all the nations,
       and we long for peace on earth.

Lord Jesus, we see in you God's commitment to humanity,
       and we rejoice in the new life that is the gift of a child's birth.

Lord Jesus, we see you in one another,
       because in your human form, we recognize our own selves.

Lord Jesus, come to us today,
       and draw us into your loving embrace.

Amen.

WORDS ABOUT MONEY

Some churches speak far too much about money, some far too little.

It is a regular theme in my preaching, not to generate income for the church but to address the discipleship demands of the gospel on our whole selves, including our bank accounts.

Our worship at Bloomsbury always includes an act of dedicating our financial giving to God, alongside the giving we offer in other ways, such as through our time, and our efforts.

These short prayers reflect something of the concerns that we bring to such a moment in our worship.

For justice

We bring our money for redistribution
        in the service of the Kingdom of God.

May justice be done,
        may the poor be blessed,
                and the wealthy justified.

Amen.

For surrendering of power

Almighty God, we dedicate our money to you.

By our financial giving through this church,
        we offer to you this tangible symbol of our power.

And as we bring our gifts,
        we surrender our control over them.

We surrender our control to you,
        and we surrender our control to one another,
as together we discern what it is
        that you would have us do with your money.

We entrust our power to others,
        and we give it away,
that your kingdom of equality, justice and peace
        may come on earth, as it is in heaven.

Amen.

For dedicating our whole lives to God

> *Inspired by the hymn 'Lord of all hopefulness'*

Lord of all hopefulness and joy,
    receive our gifts of money,
        given in gratitude for all that you have given to us.

Lord of all eagerness and faith,
    receive our efforts and our labours,
        as we offer all our days to you.

Lord of all kindliness and grace,
    receive our homes, our hospitality, and our relationships,
        as we live your love into reality.

Lord of all gentleness and calm,
    receive our whole lives, from birth to death,
        as offerings of peace given for the renewal of the world.

Amen.

For Easter Day

Lord of new life,
> receive the gifts of our lives.

Draw us from death to life,
> and draw from us the offering of our whole selves.

Receive the gifts of our time, talents and resources,
> given to you in service of your kingdom of life.

Receive the gifts given through this place,
> the gifts of our efforts,
>> as we serve one another and this city,
>
> and the gifts of our money,
>> given in the service of your greater mission
>> to bring the world to life.

Amen.

WORDS FOR THE WORLD

After the word has been proclaimed, our prayer is that we will be open to the prompting of the Spirit to draw us beyond ourselves. A response is demanded from those who have heard God's call, and so our thoughts and words turn outwards to the concerns of the wider world.

The prayers of intercession often lead us into our final hymn, as we prepare ourselves to leave the time of worship and return to the lives from which we gathered.

The first minister of Bloomsbury, William Brock, famously said that 'The Bible and The Times newspaper are the best materials for the preacher', and this concern for the affairs of the day is still very much a feature of both the preaching and prayer life of the congregation.

For racial justice

To be read by two voices.

Loving and forgiving God, we come to you today recognising that in matters of ethnicity we have no choice – we are who we have been made to be. Before you we rejoice at our diversity, and our hearts lift at your great vision of a worshipping multitude gathered from every nation, tribe, people and language. But nonetheless we recognise that our present reality is very far from this ideal.

We have each of us been shaped by different forces; some of us have been ground down, whilst others have been built up. Some of us have been worn away, or have become fractured and broken. Some of us have found life a burden rather than a joy. None of us have experienced the perfect life.

Some of us have inherited power, **whilst others of us have inherited powerlessness.**

Some of us have been born white, in a world where whiteness confers privilege. **Others of us have been born black, in a world where darker skin carries disadvantage.**

We know that this is not the world as you would have it be, but it is our world, and it has been our experience.

None of us asked for our skin colour, none of us asked to be born the heirs of oppression or oppressors, none of us asked to inherit power or powerlessness.

So before you, and in the name of Jesus Christ who loves all people equally, regardless of ethnicity, gender or social status, we come now to recommit ourselves to your vision of the world.

We come now to pray 'your kingdom come, on earth as it is in heaven', and to offer ourselves once again to live out your coming kingdom of equality and justice in our lives, in our churches, and in our communities.

And so we confess our own complicity in the status quo which divides and distorts humanity. As we pray, we ask that you will release us from guilt, and will help us to find ways of laying down the burdens we have inherited.

Help us to discover our true and rightful place within the new humanity created in Christ Jesus. All peoples together, we confess that we have sinned, and that we have fallen short of the glory of God.

We confess our failures to speak out against injustice. We confess those times when, as individuals and as churches, we have witnessed the fracturing of humanity along ethnic grounds, and yet have remained silent. We confess those times when we have been the powerful ones and have chosen to withhold that power whilst another human suffered.

We confess the sin of racist exclusion, the abuse of power to oppress and demean. May those of us who have ourselves experienced exclusion be the first to speak up for others. May we create spaces for reconciliation.

We pray for our churches. May they become places of reconciliation, where each human soul is valued, and where equality in Christ is a reality in our midst. Forgive us those times where we do not live out our calling as your people. May our churches model the new humanity of Christ to those in the communities where we live.

We pray for our communities. Where there is division, may we bring restoration. Where there is inequality may we bring justice. Where there is powerlessness may we lift up the broken hearted. Where there is damage may we bring healing.

Loving and forgiving God, hear our confession, hear the desires of our hearts to be different, grant us your forgiveness, and remake us according to the likeness of Christ.

Amen.

For the powerful and the powerless

Great God of all love, we bring before you now the world in which we live,
> and to which Christ Jesus came.
Help us to learn to see the world the way you see it,
> and teach us how to play our part
>> in the coming of your kingdom of justice and righteousness.

As we pray for those who are more powerful than we are,
> may we come to realise that all power ultimately rests with you.
And as we pray for those who are less powerful than we are,
> may we discover your image in the least and the lost.

And so we pray for your world:

We remember those who are powerful,
> those who are very sure of themselves,
> those who take pride in self-reliance.

May they recognise their needfulness of your greater call.
> May they discover that all power finds its origin
> in your powerful love for your world.

We pray for our politicians, that they may govern with integrity and justice,
> and that they will remember and represent
> those who are powerless and voiceless.

We pray for those who take important economic decisions,
> in banks, businesses and boardrooms.

May they realise that money is not the answer
> to the fundamental questions of human existence,
> however responsibly it is handled.

May they take decisions that are motivated by care
> for all people and all creation,
> rather than in the interest of short term gain.

May they be granted a vision of your in-breaking kingdom,
> learning to see the world as you see it,
> and living in accord with your loving commands.

We pray also those who are powerless: the done-upon and done-unto.

We remember those who have no power of self-determination.
    We pray for the ethnically marginalised, the asylum seekers,
    the dispossessed, and the homeless.

May they find their true home in you
    even as they struggle to find welcome from the arms of others.

May they discover in you their true sense of their value
    as dearly loved creatures of God,
and may they gain from that discovery
    the permission to see themselves as you see them
    rather than as others see them.

May they be granted a vision of your in-breaking kingdom,
    learning to see the world as you see it
    and living in accord with your loving commands.

And we also pray for ourselves.

We recognise that all too easily
    we turn our eyes from you and go our own way.

All too easily we lose your perspective on our lives,
    allowing other priorities to determine our agendas.

We ask that those of us who name you as Lord
    will be converted not just to the risen Christ,
but also to the church which is his body,
    and to the world for which he died.

May we live in our lives the truth of the gospel of good news for all.

May we be granted a vision of your in-breaking kingdom,
    learning to see the world as you see it
    and living in accord with your loving commands.

Amen.

For living water

Great God of eternal love,
        we bring before you now those places in our lives,
        and in our world, where it seems as if you are absent.

We recognise that sometimes life can take a path
        of desolation that none would choose,
and that in the midst of the wilderness of the world,
        the reality of your love can seem a distant memory of a lost dream.

God of living water, we pray now for those
        whose world is more wilderness than fertility.
We think of those who live in places
        where the land does not sustain the population with adequate food,
        where children are malnourished and adults go to bed hungry.

We pray for those who develop sustainable and productive agriculture,
        bringing life from the barren land,
and for those who dig wells and supply water to bring life
        to those who dwell in the desert places.
May those who are hungry and thirsty find nourishment,
        and may it come to them as life-giving water
        from the deep well of your eternal love.

God of living water, we pray for those
        who hunger and thirst for righteousness;
for those who find themselves living under oppressive political systems
        that deny them freedom of thought, speech and action.

We think of those who are not free to choose their religion,
        for those who are not free to act according to their conscience,
        for those who are routinely denied righteousness
            by the corrupt legal systems that should defend them.

We pray for those who work for freedom for all, for organisations such as
        Amnesty International, *Liberty*, and *Action by Christians Against Torture*.
May those who are oppressed find freedom,
        and may it come to them as life-giving water
        from the deep well of your eternal love.

FAITH IN DOUBT

God of living water, we pray now for those who are denied truth,
    for those who are deceived by ideologies of hatred,
    and those who are raised on stories of sectarianism.

We pray for those countries
    where civil war and systemic violence have become normalised,
    and we think particularly of …

We also pray for those caught up in the web of politicised posturing,
    as innocent people find themselves entwined
    in the machinery of international politics.

We pray for those who speak truth into such situations,
    for journalists who put their lives at risk
    to tell the stories that would otherwise go untold.

We pray that truth will set people free,
    that those who have been deceived
    will hear the truth that all are equal in your sight,
and that the truth will come to them as life-giving water
    from the deep well of your eternal love.

Great God of water in the wilderness,
    Great God of eternal life-giving water,
Come to those who thirst,
    come to those who are oppressed,
        come to those who are deceived.

We pray that you will bring the sustenance, freedom, and truth,
    from the deep well of your eternal love.

And as we pray, we commit ourselves,
    to sharing with you in the task of bringing new life
    to those living in the valley of the shadow of death.

For the sake of Jesus Christ we pray.

Amen.

For light, life, and love

Great God of all light, life, and love,
> we come now to pray for a world where love is so often lacking,
>> where so many people live in darkness,
>> and where life is not experienced in all its fullness.

We pray for those places where your activity can clearly be seen.

We pray this day for our families,
> and we rejoice that good and loving parenting
> is a reflection of your great love for all your children.

Be with those who are parents,
> and may they know the joy of seeing their children grow
> into independence and maturity.

We lift up before you especially those children
> who live with violent, abusive, or inadequate parenting,
and we pray for all those entrusted with ensuring the safeguarding
> of the young and vulnerable in our society and our community.

We pray for all those who this past week
> have celebrated love through entering into married life.

We rejoice that love, faithfulness and commitment are gifts from you,
> and we give thanks for those whose experience of love
> is one of equality and mutuality.

We are grateful for those moments in our own lives
> where we have been especially conscious
> of your presence this week.

Help us to see your love at work in our lives.

FAITH IN DOUBT

We pray for those who are blind to your great love.

We think of those who struggle to comprehend anything positive
        in their experience of life;
for those who live with mental illness, depression, and anger,
        and for those who find that their inner eye remains closed
            to the goodness of creation,
        despite their desperate desire to find a path to the light.

Reach out your healing hand
        to those who live under the shadow of despair,
and give the gift of hope that comes through Christ.

We pray also for those who see you
        as a negative, violent, and vengeful God,
        rather than as a God of life, light, and love.

We think of those whose own experiences of negativity in their family life
        has shaped for them a negative vision of you.

We pray for those who are forever trying
        to please an implacable and unforgiving God,
for those who live with guilt and hurt
        and find no forgiveness and healing when they pray,
for those who live in fear and not in love.

Great God of love, open their eyes to you
        as the source of eternal love and peace,
and come to them through your son
        to speak words of life,
        to bring healing and wholeness,
        and restoration of relationships.

FAITH IN DOUBT

We pray for those places where you are active but we cannot see it.

Sometimes it can be hard to discern
    the shape of your kingdom in our world.

When we think of those places torn apart
    by war, famine, and natural disaster,
we struggle to comprehend how it can be that you are a God of love.

Lord, we pray for those who live in the midst of such situations,
    and we ask that they will be especially conscious of you
    with them in the midst of their suffering.

Great God of the cross, be with those who are in agony,
    and may it be true for them that the life that you bring
    can redeem even the horrors of death.

We pray for those places where you are active but people deny or oppose your activity.

We pray for those who are wedded to ideas that seem unshakeable,
    until they are shaken by you.

We pray for those who claim your name
    to promote restrictive dogma and oppressive religion.

We pray for those of all faiths and none who deny your great love
    through their words, actions, and deeds.

Great God of all creation,
    we rejoice that you are not restricted by creed or confession,
and we know that you can open a path to the light of your love,
    even into the darkest corners of the human heart.

We pray for those who run from the light,
    because they have become bound to deeds of darkness.
Come, Lord Jesus, bring light to our world.

Forgive us our sins, as we forgive those who sin against us,
    lead us to wholeness and restoration,
and may our eyes be opened to your kingdom breaking in upon the world.

Amen.

For seeing the world differently

Great God of all times, all places, and all people,
>we begin our prayers by remembering
>those who have gone before us.

We lift before you in mixed remembrance
>those who have shaped us,
>those who have taught us,
>those who have made us what and who we are.

We think of parents and grandparents,
>teachers and Sunday school teachers,
>friends, enemies, mentors and ministers.

For both good and bad, we recognise the influences
>they have had in shaping us,
and in the midst of the complexities of our own lives,
>we recognise and hold before you
>the complexities of the lives of others.

May we find gratitude where gratitude is appropriate,
>may we offer thanksgiving where thanksgiving is fitting,
and may we find forgiveness and reconciliation in unexpected places.

For that which has gone before, for that which we cannot change,
>we offer our diverse prayers, and seek your gracious forgiveness.

By your grace, and by the intervention of your Holy Spirit,
>we give thanks that we are more than the sum of our parts,
and we rejoice that the realities of our lives
>transcend the heritage of our history.

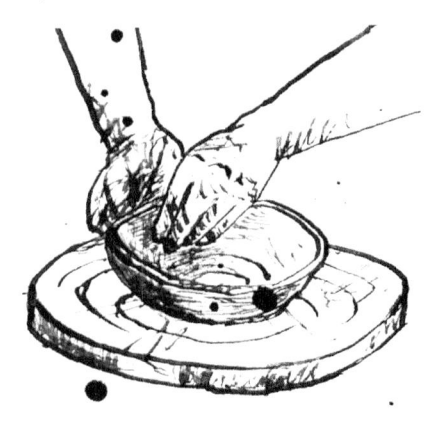

Great God of all times, all places, and all people,
>we ask that you will meet us in the complexities of this day,

by the transforming, resurrecting, and life-giving presence
>of your risen son Jesus Christ.

May we know in our time, and our place, your healing and forgiveness,
>may our relationships with others
>>be transformative moments of grace,
>and may our choices and activities
>>reflect your love for each created being.

Forgive us for those times when we think our days are unimportant,
>and may we know the eternal value
>>that you place on each moment;
>the significance you attach to each action and interaction.

And forgive us for those days
>when we think our lives matter more than they do;

may we know the humility of living
>that comes from following your example,

as we learn to reject the whispers of self-aggrandizement
>and the deceptions of our egos.

And so we come now to pray for those around us,
>for those who affect us, and for those whom we affect.

We pray for our families and friends,
>for the intricate networks of relationships within which we exist,
>and to which we contribute.

May those who mourn, know comfort,
>may those who are struggling, find peace,

may those who are hungry, find sustenance,
>and may those who are poor, find blessing.

In a moment of silence we hold names before you,
>in faith that a world where a prayer has been offered
>is a world where transformation is coming into being.

Silence…

Great God of all times, all places, and all people,
    we pray now for the world beyond our sphere of influence.
For countries we have never visited,
    and people we will never meet.

We pray for Christians who are persecuted,
    and for those who persecute them.

We pray for the political leaders who seek peace,
    and for those who seek conflict.

We pray for …

May the current fruit of violence and conflict,
    that is daily born from the vine of history
        in these troubled nations,
    be transformed the fruit of peace, justice, and reconciliation

We pray for your world.

Great God of all times, all places, and all people,
    help us to discern truth in the midst of lies,
    and to have the courage to speak out for truth.

May we resist the tendency to scapegoat others,
    and learn instead to see where true suffering lies.

May we learn to see others as you see them.
    May we learn to see your world as you see it.
        May we learn to see ourselves as you see us.

Great God of past, present, and future,
    may we be part of your in-breaking kingdom
    of peace, justice, and reconciliation,
as together as your redeemed people,
    we live out your love for all people, in all places.

Amen.

For the whole earth

Great God of the whole earth, we come today
> to bring before you the needs of this planet.

And we do so trusting that you are the God of Aleppo,
> and the God of the West Bank;
that you are the God of Ukraine, and the God of Yemen;
> the God of this city, and the God of this church.

We trust that you are God of the environment, and of the climate;
> that you are God of the marginalised, and the victimised;
God of the poor, and the suffering;
> God of the well and the wealthy;
God of the safe and the secure.

We trust that you are God of the whole earth,
> and we trust that you are our God, and we are your people.

And so it is in trust that we your people, cry out to you
> that the world is not the way that it should be.

Every day we see people diminished and distorted in their humanity.

From those living in war zones
> and being used as weapons in fights that are not of their making,
to those dropping bombs and piloting drones,
> to those holding civilians hostage
> > to ideologies of hatred and desperation,
to those who could negotiate peace
> but whose national interest is better served by war.

We remember the example of Jesus
> who sat and ate with outsiders and sinners,
who received hospitality
> and gave friendship across borders and boundaries,
and we commit ourselves to living differently,
> to seeing the person behind their presentation of themselves,
to finding the image of the divine in each created being.

Help us to open ourselves to those
    who worship in different ways to us.

Release us from suspicion of the other,
    and from fear of difference.
May we learn to build bridges
    across divisions of faith, ethnicity, and origin.

Open our eyes to the systems of oppression that enslave humanity.

Through our prayers for others
    may we find within ourselves the commitment and the courage
to stand against those powers and principalities of wealth and patriarchy
    that subjugate women, constrict men, exclude children,
    disadvantage the marginalised, and impoverish the vulnerable.

And in a world where death always seems to get the final word on life,
    we recommit ourselves to the one
    who brings life to the living and hope to the dying.

And so we stand in prayer alongside those who are sick,
    those who are diminished through dementia,
    those who are living with terminal illness.

We pray for our friends, and for our families, and for ourselves.

May those who need courage be granted it,
    may those who seek peace discover it.
May those who long for rest find it.

Great God of the whole earth,
    may we find our purpose and completion in you.

Amen.

For praying with raised eyes, hearts, hands, and voices.

Inspired by the hymn 'Now Thank We All Our God'

Great God of peace and love,
    we turn to you now with thanksgiving in our hearts
    to pray for the world you died to save.

In the cross of your son Jesus Christ,
    we catch a vision of the end of violence,
    and the cessation of suffering.

As we **lift our eyes** to the cross in thankful worship,
    we see all the pain and hurt of this world
    present in the broken body of our saviour.

So help us to lift our eyes with courage,
    to fearlessly face the forces of evil
    that continually seek to mar your image in humanity.

May we see with your eyes
    those systems of oppression that masquerade as truth,
and may we learn from you
    how to see through the propaganda that would deceive us.

So we name before you the ideologies of division
    that distort and divide humanity.

From racism to sexism,
    from socio-economic bias to homophobia,
we see people divided one from another,
    with families fractured and societies segmented.

And we commit ourselves to living differently,
    to modelling in our midst the unity that comes through Christ,
    where all are equal and loved by you.

And as we lift our eyes to the cross in thankful worship,
    we ask that you will open our eyes to the alternative future
    that you are bringing into being in and through us your people.

So in thankful worship for all that you have done through the cross,
    we lift **our hearts, our hands, and our voices.**

FAITH IN DOUBT

Keep us from hardened **hearts** and compassion fatigue.

As we hear the news each day,
        with seemingly unending stories
        of suffering from around the world,
it is all too easy for us to close our hearts to the litany of sadness,
        and to focus on our more immediate, more parochial concerns.

So open our hearts and drive us to prayer
        as we bring before you those close to us and those far away.
We pray especially for …,
        and for all those affected by terrorist activity over recent months.

We pray for those who work for peace,
        and for those who have to try to keep the peace.
We ask that they will have the courage and creativity
        to explore other paths to a future
            where the spirals of violence are disrupted,
        and where all people, on all sides, have their humanity restored.

We pray also for those near and dear to us,
        and we hold before you our friends and our families.
And we ask for your grace in all our relationships,
        that we might live in love with one another.

So with open hearts, we lift up our **hands** in thankful worship,
        offering our best efforts to the service of your coming kingdom.

With hands open to welcome the stranger,
        and open to give as we have received,
        we offer our daily labours before you.

From the workplace to the home,
        may all that we do reflect your love for all people.

From those whom we touch to the items we hold,
        may our lives become an offering of thankful worship.

May we be the hands of Jesus in this world,
        and may all that we do be honouring to him.

And so with eyes open to the cross, with hearts open to the world,
> and with hands lifted for service,
>> we raise our **voices** in thankful praise.

And as we name your son Jesus Christ as Lord,
> we speak and sing into being an alternative reality
where all other claims to power are brought under the lordship of Christ.

As we worship you, and you alone,
> we unleash upon the earth the antidote to idolatry,
and through the proclamation of your salvation
> the way is opened for people to find release
>> from their fears, their guilt, and their sin.

So help us to speak truth to power,
> to raise up our voices in advocacy
>> for those who cannot speak for themselves,
> to speak comfort for those who mourn,
>> and words of love to those who hear only condemnation.

In thankful praise we raise our voices,
> we lift up our hands, we open our hearts,
> and we lift our eyes to the cross.

Receive our worship, great God of peace and love.

Amen.

For love, light, and life

Great God of all love, light, and life,
> we come to you today in deep gratitude,
> that you have made us to be your dearly loved children.

We thank you that you call us by name,
> and that you invite us to a new identity, a new purpose, a new life.

And so on this day, as every day, we come to be born again,
> to discover afresh our being as your children,
> to find renewal, and to know forgiveness.

May our lived experience of this day
> reflect the unconditional love
> with which you embrace each moment of our lives.

May our hopes and our dreams
> find completion in your love,
and may our fears and our pain
> find comfort in your eternal embrace.

Help us in our relationships with those we meet,
> to be ambassadors of your love,
> which is poured out in Christ for the whole world.

May we be peacemakers,
> may we be comforters,
may we be those who have the courage
> to speak out against injustice,
and the conviction to act to bring the reality of your coming kingdom
> one step closer to those who cannot yet see it, let alone live it.

And so we pray for those whose lives are lived enslaved
> to powers that distort and demean your image in humanity.

We pray for those who, through their actions,
> cause wounds to innocent flesh.

We pray for those who know what they are doing,
> and for those who know not what they do.

FAITH IN DOUBT

And in humility we know that as we pray for others,
>   we pray also for ourselves,
because we are all complicit in the shared sins of humanity.

We recognise that your great love for us
>   is merely one facet of your great love for all,
and that your outstretched arms that embrace us as your children,
>   also extend your love to all peoples, in all countries.

And so we pray for those places in your world
>   where war and violence are most obvious.

We pray today for … in all its complexity,
>   with wrong on so many sides.
And we dare to pray for peace, for an end to fighting,
>   and for a new start for that nation.

From those affected directly by recent events,
>   to those countless millions of refugees
>   seeking a new and peaceful life
>   away from their place of birth,
>   we see suffering and desperation and death,
>   and we long for your new world
>   of peace and justice for those so affected.

In repentance we mourn those deaths
>   that have occurred this week in our name,
and we recognise that guilt spreads its net far and wide.

Forgive us, forgive those who choose death,
>   forgive those who know not what they do,
>   and those who know exactly what they are doing.

May your kingdom come, may your will be done.
>   May life triumph over death,
>   and light shine in the world's darkness.

And so we pray with gratitude for aid workers
>   and humanitarian agencies,
for negotiators and peacekeepers.

FAITH IN DOUBT

We pray for those who are seeking to bring an end
        to the spirals of violence,
and who need courage to question the assumption
        that fighting is the way to achieve peace.

We pray for a renewal of community,
        as people discover the common humanity we all share in Christ,
which binds us to one another
        across all borders of colour, creed, or identity.

We pray for our leaders and politicians,
        for those who we asked to take these decisions on our behalf.

We give thanks for all those who are willing to stand for public office.
        Give them wisdom, selflessness,
        and an unswerving commitment to the common good.
Help us to make good choices in our voting,
        as we play our part in the shared goal
        of living well together in society.

And finally, we pray for ourselves.

We know that the new world that you are bringing into being
        begins with us, today.

Help us to live the reality of what it means to be your children.

Help us to hold onto your great love
        that we have experienced in our lives,
in the faithful expectation and hope
        that that same love extends to all people, in all places.

Help us to lay aside any special claim we may feel we have
        on our identity as your children;
may we see you in the other, discover you in the stranger,
        and meet you in the enemy.

May your kingdom come, may your will be done,
        on earth as it is in heaven.

Amen.

For the Body of Christ

Great God of the whole earth,
    you call us to be your body.

And so today, as your body gathered in this place,
    we offer our whole selves to your service.

May we be knit together by your Spirit,
    so that our common life reflects your calling and your will.

Direct our thoughts, words, and deeds
    in ways that make real in this world
        the eternal truth of your coming kingdom.

Teach our eyes to see the world as you see it,
    rather than as the world wants to be seen.

May we learn to see through the insidious propaganda
    that so readily dominates human relationships
        from the interpersonal to the international.

May we learn that the 'other' is also a child of God,
    as deeply loved and valued as we are ourselves.

From the abstract refugee, migrant, and asylum seeker,
    to the person we find most difficult in our day to day lives,
        may we discover you in those whom we fear.

And so we pray for those who help us to see.

We pray for journalists, for opinion formers,
    for politicians, and for bloggers.

We thank you for fearless truth telling,
    and we pray for integrity
        for all those who show others what to believe.

We thank you for the freedom of speech that we enjoy in this country,
    and we ask for your wisdom
        as we discern where we should direct our own eyes.

FAITH IN DOUBT

May we look not only to our own interests,
    but also to the interests of others.

And as we have seen, so we must do.
    Teach us, living Lord, where we should take our stand.

May we be released from the compulsion
    to aggressively defend our own territory,
and instead may we learn what it means
    to stand on justice and righteousness and truth.

As the firm ground of our certainties shifts beneath us,
    may we learn how to walk new paths
    of collaboration and cooperation.

So we pray for our 'traditional' enemies,
    for those whom we instinctively stand against,
and we ask that in the new world of your Spirit,
    enemies may become friends
    reaching out across borders previously uncrossed.

And so we pray for …
    May peace and justice and righteousness prevail.

We pray also for those who take their stand
    on issues of moral or theological certainty,
    and in so doing exclude others from your love.

Grant us again a vision of your universal kingdom
    which recognises no divisions and transcends all borders.

And as we negotiate the changing territory of the world,
    we pray that you will direct our actions.

May the works of our hands be acceptable in your sight.
    May we build friendships and not enmities.

May we reach out in love and acceptance
    to those whom others would push away.

May we become your body,
> extending a welcome to all, in your name;
bringing food to the hungry,
> clothing to the naked, and healing to the sick.

May our hands be generous in your service,
> releasing our time, talents and money
> > to the service of your kingdom.

So we pray for all those with whom we partner
> as we reach out to the vulnerable and hurting of this world.

Great God of us all, teach us to live in love,
> to stand in hope, and to act with justice.

For the sake of your kingdom.

Amen.

For victims of sexual violence.

God of the cross, we turn to you
        from a world of weakness and violence.

With heavy hearts and troubled souls
        we recognise what we should always have known;
that the capacity for violence
        lies deep within the human condition,
        and affects each of us in different ways.

We pray today for the victims of sexual violence,
        for those who are abused, dis-voiced, and silenced.

Bring comfort where there is hurt,
        bring healing where there is harm,
bring peace where there is chaos,
        bring justice where there is none.

We pray for social workers and the police,
        and all entrusted with the care
        of those who have been harmed.
Give them attentiveness in listening and strength in action.

We pray for counsellors and therapists,
        and for all who offer companionship
        to those making painful journeys of the soul.
May they have the ability to discern the right words to offer,
        and the wisdom to know when to keep silence.

We pray for prison guards and probation officers,
        and for all those who deal daily
        with people who have committed violent acts.
May they never lose sight of the humanity of each human soul,
        and may rehabilitation always be the goal.

FAITH IN DOUBT

We pray for all those who are victims
> of unseen, unacknowledged, and unreported sexual violence;
from the backstreets of our city,
> to the closed doors of respectable houses.

We pray for children who witness assault in the home,
> and for all those who are powerless
> to protect those whom they love.

God of the cross,
> your response to the pain and hurt of the world,
has always been to enter fully
> into the depths of darkest humanity.

So come now, into the darkness of our times and our lives.

Come to bring release from fear and hurt,
> come to bring comfort and healing of the soul and body,
come to bring courage in the face of terror,
> come to bring the good news of the cross.

We offer our prayers in the name of Jesus,
> our friend and saviour,

Amen.

For justice and peace

Great God of all love, all compassion, all hope, and all joy,
        we come before you today mindful of the needs of others,
and longing that your gospel of justice and peace
        would be good news for all people, in all places.

And yet we know that there is so much still to do,
        we know that darkness lurks in so many places,
        we know that human hearts remain turned from you,
and that there are many who suffer
        because people of faith remain inactive or silent.

We are particularly grieved when we think
        that there are those who long to know
                your redeeming and transforming presence in their lives,
        but who are kept from you by the people who bear your name.

As we consider the ways in which we welcome people
        into this community of your people here in this church,
we ask for your forgiveness
        for those times when our actions or inactions
have caused people to be turned away
        from finding you in and through us.

Give us a desire to live differently, to welcome all in your name,
        and a hope that transcends despair.

Sometimes, when we consider the needs
        of a hurting and damaged world,
it can feel as though we are weighed down
        with the responsibilities we have taken upon ourselves.

The task before us feels too great,
        and the efforts we make too insignificant.

So Lord we ask that you will restore unto us the joy of our salvation,
        may we rediscover in you the lightness of living
                that drew us to you in the first place,
        and which continues to draw others
                into your love, forgiveness, and renewal.

FAITH IN DOUBT

May your people in this place be beacons of light and hope,
    discovering joy in the midst of despair,
    comfort in the face of grief,
    and faith that transcends all discouragements.

It is in this spirit of hope that we come now
    to pray for the needs of our world,
confident that you are at work in the world in and through your people
    bringing new life and resurrection hope.

And so we pray those who live in other countries,
    for those impacted by the effects of climate change,
    and for those affected by war.

We think of those who have lost their homes to floods,
    those who have been displaced by armies and ideologies,
    and those who do not have enough to eat.

We pray for the aid agencies, and peacekeeping forces,
    as they seek to bring help and alleviate suffering.

May our love for you drive us to a concern for others
    that takes action in prayerful generosity.

As we think of the political situation in our own country,
    we recognise the need for finding a way forwards
    that safeguards the most vulnerable in our society.

We pray for our political leaders,
    and we ask that they will not lose sight
        of the impact their decisions will have on those with low incomes,
            for whom any economic downturn
                or reduction in benefits can be catastrophic.

We thank you for the work done by the Christian churches in this country
    to speak truth to power
and for the way our national leaders hold before our decision makers
    the needs of those who may not have a voice
    to speak for themselves.

FAITH IN DOUBT

We thank you for the *Baptist Union*,
    for the work of the *Faith and Society Team*,
        and the *Joint Public Issues Team*
    as they advocate on issues of justice.

We pray particularly for our General Secretary,
    and ask that you will impart stamina, and joy, and peace.

And finally, Lord, we pray for ourselves.

Help us, as individuals and as a church,
    to know what it is to live into being
    the joyful good news of your in-breaking kingdom.

May we learn to love one another more
    and may we learn to love you more.

From our sharing in love may we be motivated
    to take action together as faith becomes deeds,
to see your kingdom come, on earth, as it is in heaven.

All this we pray in the name of our saviour Jesus Christ,

Amen.

For love, mercy, and justice

Great God of eternal love, everlasting mercy, and endless justice,
>we bring before you today the needs of our world.

Nation lifts up arms against nation,
>and the innocent suffer and die
>in the pursuit of ideologies of nationalism.

We pray for Palestine, and we pray for Israel,
>and we ask for mercy and justice for all those who suffer,
>and we long for an end to division, segregation, and violence.

We also remember before you the wider powers at play in that region,
>especially the United States, Saudia Arabia, Syria, and Iran,
and we faithfully hope for the day when voices speaking peace
>will triumph over those calling for further bloodshed.

We pray for the Yemen,
>for those who are dying in war, and for those who are starving;
>and we particularly remember those
>>working to bring humanitarian relief.

We pray for Afghanistan,
>cauldron of competing tensions,
and we remember all those
>caught in conflicts beyond their making.

We pray for South Sudan,
>trying to find a path to peace, but living with a legacy of horror.

We hold before you all those who have been forced to fight
>and we ask that former child soldiers
>>will find ways to build new lives,
>even as their victims grieve their actions.

We pray also for those living with the impact of climate change,
>and we recognise that the global injustices of carbon consumption
>fall disproportionately on the poorest people on the planet.

FAITH IN DOUBT

We lift the longings of our hearts for a new world
      where care for creation and care for the poor
        are at the heart of our politics rather than side-lined to the margins.

We rejoice in the freedoms we have,
      and we give thanks for the good things in our lives.

We offer our prayers as expressions
      of our desire for your coming kingdom,
and we offer our lives as witness and testimony
      to the new world we dream of.

Help us to live faithfully, and may the answers to our prayers
      begin with us.

Amen.

For a fresh vision of God's coming kingdom

Loving God of all the earth, we come before you today
    seeking a fresh vision of your coming kingdom.

Help us to see the world as it is,
    and not how it wants to be seen.
Teach us to pray for the world as it is,
    that it might become the world that it should be.
Give us new ways of telling your story,
    so that truth can echo down the millennia to our world today.

We pray for all those who are deceived by the propaganda of empire,
    who find themselves worshipping the contemporary beasts
    of idolatrous, corrupt and powerful institutions.

From corporations to countries, from tribalism to nationalism,
    from destructive theologies to pervasive ideologies,
we pray that truth will speak to power,
    and that people trapped in cycles of hatred
        will discover the all-embracing love
    that you reveal to any who have eyes to see and ears to hear.

We pray for those who live with conflict,
    facing daily the threat of physical harm
    to their property, person, and family.
We pray for people who are oppressed because of their ethnicity,
    and because of the satanic lie
    that one life is worth more than another.

We name …,
    and we ask for the abiding peace of Christ
    to be made known in those countries.

We pray for Christians who live in places
        where the churches of Christ are persecuted,
where the might of oppression
        threatens to overwhelm the truth of the gospel.

We think particularly of places
        where it is illegal or dangerous to be Christian,
        or profess publicly faith n Christ,

and we name North Korea, Afghanistan, Somalia, Libya, Pakistan,
        Sudan, Eritrea, Yemen, Iran, and Syria.

We thank you for those mission organisations
        that bring the good news of Christ
to countries such as these, and we pray for them,
        and for those who speak out
        to highlight persecution around the world.

We give thanks for *BMS World Mission*, *Christian Aid*,
        Open Doors, and *Release International*,

We pray for those individuals of power who do great evil in the world,
        for the Neros of our time.
We pray for those who are adversaries of truth,
        for the Satans of our world.

May those who speak hatred and lies,
        and who sow division and dissent,
        and who misuse power for their own ends,
be unmasked and held to account for their actions.

We pray for our own political leaders,
    that they will resist the seductions of power,
and ever hold before them the common good
    of the people they represent.

We pray especially for the Prime Minister of this country,
    that they will lead well, defend the weak,
    and protect the vulnerable.

We thank you for organisations such as
    the *Joint Public Issues Team*, *Citizens UK*, and …,
    which work with churches to bring about justice in our society.

We recommit ourselves to being part of the answer to our prayers,
    as we seek to live into being the kingdom for which we pray.

Give us a vision of your great love for all people,
    and may we be faithful in all things.

Amen.

For wholeness for the world

Loving God of Unity and Peace,
        we rejoice that in you we are brought to wholeness,
        and that through your love we are healed of our divisions.

As we come now to pray for your world,
        we hold before you in our prayers a world divided,
a world where the glorious spectrum of human existence
        is reduced to simple binary choices
        which lead to division and violence.

And we ask for your forgiveness for our complicity
        in simplistic and reductionist ideologies of isolation.

So we pray for a world of **us and them**,
        a world of othering and exclusion,
        a world of tribalism and localism.

We confess the fears we hold in our own hearts,
        the suspicions we have of those who are not like us,
the indifference to those who differ from us
        in ethnicity, culture, or language.

We also confess the prejudices that divide our society,
        with fear of the other, and a desire to exclude the stranger,
        setting so many aspects of our national narrative.

And so we pray for refugees, for asylum seekers, for economic migrants,
        and we pray for those who are the descendants
        of historic immigration.

We pray for those caught up in inherited cycles of poverty and violence,
        for those who feel coerced to carry weapons from an early age,
        and for those who are prey to gangs
            and organised crime networks.

FAITH IN DOUBT

Give strength to those who work for reconciliation between peoples
       in our city, and in our country.

Give clarity to those who speak up for people
       who have no voice to speak up for themselves.

Give tenacity to those who seek to welcome refugees,
       who arrive reliant on the hospitality of others.

We pray for a world of us and them.

We pray also for a world of **male and female**,
       a world of othering and exclusion,
       a world of simplistic division and binary choices.

We confess the fears we hold in our own hearts,
       fears of the other and the unknown,
       fears of emotions and desires suppressed and repressed.

We confess the prejudices that divide our society,
       with stereotypes imposed out of fear or ignorance,
       and reinforced for financial gain by corporations and businesses.

Help us, as your people who gather in this place,
       to discover and rejoice
              in the glorious spectrum of humanity that you have made,
       and to learn to trust other people's stories,
              even where they feel different to our own.

We pray for all those who have faced isolation and prejudice with churches,
       because of their experience of their own gender.

We pray for those who have the courage to speak out,
       to tell truth in the face of misinformation,
       and to model in their own lives
       the truth of your love for all people.

FAITH IN DOUBT

We pray for the work of *One Body One Faith*,
        of the *Two:23 Network*, and of *Stonewall*.
Give strength to those who, in your name,
        challenge homophobia, biphobia and transphobia.

We pray for a world of us and them.
We pray for a world of male and female.

And in all these our prayers we recognise that our language
        is itself inadequate to express and match
        the intent you have for your people.

We are fallen,
        and the way we speak of you and of one another is also fallen.
When we name your creation,
        we name it at best provisionally.

So we keep speaking binary into existence,
        asserting *mine* over *yours*, and *us* over *them*.

The confusion of our language,
        with its inadequacies of pronouns and gender,
reminds us of the confusion we live with,
        and with which we must struggle to come to terms.

So we thank you for those who help us evolve our ways of speaking,
        we thank you for hymn writers and liturgists,
        we thank you for poets and preachers,
we thank you for those who challenge us
        to speak a new world into existence.

Give us open hearts and minds,
        that we might better express the diversity of your creation.

Amen.

For those who live in isolation

God of comfort and community, God of business and solitude,
> God of laughter and loneliness, we pray for one another.

We commit to your presence all those known to us who live alone,
> or experience the isolation of fractured relationships.

Give us the courage and compassion
> to offer the welcoming word and a listening ear.

May the community of your church be made real in our midst,
> as we care for one another.

Amen.

For living life in all its fullness

"Holy, holy, holy, Lord God the Almighty, who was and is and is to come."

Eternal God of past, present, and future,
> we entrust the days of our lives to your love,

and ask that we will be granted the grace to live life in all its fullness.

May we care for others as we care for ourselves,
> and may we learn to love you more with every day,
> so that our lives may display more of your love to others.

Amen.

For new life in the face of violence

To him who loves us and freed us from our sins by his blood, and made us to be a kingdom, priests serving his God and Father, to him be glory and dominion forever and ever. Amen. (Revelation 1:5-6)

Lord Jesus Christ, son of the living God,
        we come before you today as your beloved people.

We thank you that you have called us by name,
        and that because of your calling
        we have become part of your great family,
joining those from every tribe and language and nation as your holy people.

In a world of violence and bloodshed,
        we recognize our own complicity in the sins of the world.

We acknowledge that, directly or indirectly,
        we are party to the systems of oppression and domination
        which feed and perpetuate the global cycles of hatred and poverty.

We confess our implicit complicity in corruption,
        and with horror we see the blood stains on our own hands.

The blood of our sisters and brothers
        cries out from the earth for justice.

And so we turn to the cross as the end of violence,
        and there we encounter you, Lord Jesus Christ,
        our lord and our saviour.

In your shed blood we see the blood of the innocent,
        the blood of the martyrs,
        the blood of the oppressed,
        the blood of the enslaved.

In the horror of the cross we meet the worst excesses of humanity,
        and find the end result of our own sinfulness.

And yet, at the point of condemnation, at the moment of judgment,
> we encounter mercy and forgiveness.

At your cross our guilt is atoned.
> By your blood we are freed from our sins.

The stench of death becomes the promise of new life.

So, resurrected Lord, breathe new life into us today.
> Make us and remake us to be the people of your kingdom.

May we be those who, through naming you as Lord,
> find freedom and forgiveness.

May we, as the redeemed people of God,
> be those who draw others into your kingdom
> of grace and forgiveness.

To you be glory and dominion forever and ever.

Amen.

For the politics of our time

Great God of all the earth,
        in you are found the full riches of our human experience,
and you call us to live our lives
        out of the richness of your self-giving in Christ.

So may our lives reflect the life that you bring to the world.
        May we learn what it is to put others before ourselves.

May we learn what it means to see your image in each created human soul,
        however marred and distorted that image has become
        as a result of human sinfulness.

And so as we come to pray for our world,
        we do so aware of the common humanity we share with all people,
        and in the light of your greater call
        to forgiveness and reconciliation.

May our prayers shape a world where self is made less,
        and where generosity and grace are grown.

So we pray for victims of terrorist activity around the world,
        and we are aware that within the lifetime of some of us here today,
        it was our own country that brought death
            to the streets of European cities,
            even as others brought death to ours.

But we know that terror can turn to peace,
        just as peace can turn to war.

So we pray for international peacemakers, for politicians and civil servants,
        for lawyers and judges, and doctors and medics,
and all those who strive for reconciliation and healing.

We pray for our own country's relationship with its neighbours.

May we not lose our sense of common humanity,
        where each person is valued regardless of creed or ethnicity.
May we, as your church, have the courage to speak out for justice for all,
        and for reconciliation in place of conflict.

FAITH IN DOUBT

And as our nation lifts its eyes to the wider global stage,
> we pray for the United States of America.

We thank you for the many ways in which American culture at its best
> has contributed positively to the world,
>> for their values of justice, equality, and fairness.

But we also recognise those voices
> that would promote hatred, fear, and self-interest,
and we recognise them
> because they echo voices we hear in our own country,
>> and, in our darker moments, in our own hearts too.

May your love and justice triumph in our lives,
> in our country, and in our world.

We believe that your giving of yourself
> in Christ on the cross was for the whole world,
>> for Jew, Christian, Muslim, atheist, Hindu, and Buddhist.

We believe that the cross offers a way to end violence
> as you reach out to those of all political persuasions
and show a new and better way of being human,
> one where our lives mirror your self-giving.

And so may the revolution of love and peace begin with us.
> May we be those who show to the world
>> what it means to put the other first,
>> to see your divine image in each created soul,
> and to live out the truth that in you
>> are found the full riches of our human experience.

Amen.

WORDS INSPIRED BY SCRIPTURAL TEXTS

At the heart of worship is scripture, through which God speaks, inspires, calls, and reprimands. Sometimes the words of our prayers for the world are rooted deeply in the scriptural text that has given shape to the sermon and the rest of the service.

These prayers that follow acknowledge that debt, and are offered not simply as further prayers of intercession, but also as an invitation to revisit the scriptures that inspired them, and reflect on how they continue to speak to our current context in new ways.

For justice to grow

Inspired by the parables of the seeds in Mark 4.24-34

**Your kingdom come, your will be done
on earth, as in heaven.**

Great God of small beginnings and hidden revolutions,
    we bring before you now the needs of our world,
    and the concerns of our hearts.

We pray for those countries
    where peace and justice are threatened and diminished,
where those who would seek
    to live the values of your dawning kingdom are persecuted,
and where violence and fear
    control the hearts and minds of citizens and subjects.

We recommit ourselves to the ideal that,
    in the name of Christ, it does not have to be this way.
And so we pray for those small and subversive voices
    who dare to speak your alternative into being.

We pray for those seeking peace between unreconciled peoples,
    for those who stand up for values of justice and equality,
for those who live out in their lives
    the conviction that all are created equal.
We pray especially for… .

**Your kingdom come, your will be done
on earth, as in heaven.**

We pray for those countries where economic circumstances
> are leading to inequality and instability,
where the rich and powerful are acting in self-interest
> while the poor and vulnerable are once again
> required to make the 'necessary' sacrifices.

We recommit ourselves to the ideal that,
> in the name of Christ, it does not have to be this way.
And so we pray for those small and subversive voices
> who dare to speak your alternative into being.

We pray for those who are advocating
> the alternative economics of the kingdom of God,
for those who promote the kingdom values
> of equality and of care for the disadvantaged,
for microfinance initiatives, for credit unions,
> cooperatives and friendly societies.
We pray especially for... .

Your kingdom come, your will be done
on earth, as in heaven.

We pray for those who lead our own country.
> For our politicians and community leaders.
May values of truth and honesty triumph,
> and not be lost to the value of spin and self-interest.

We pray for those seeking to see our cities transformed,
> for street pastors walking the risky path of our night streets.
We pray for those who champion restorative justice
> in the face of the hard logic of retribution and punishment.

Your kingdom come, your will be done
on earth, as in heaven.

We pray for our church.
>> May we be delivered from self-deception.
May we be resistant to the insidious mythologies of success and status,
>> and instead may we become the dissident disciples
who live by the alternative stories spoken in the name of Christ
>> in the face of those false truths that appear so self-evident.

May we have the imagination to hold lightly to our certainties,
>> and may we be ready to creatively lay aside our fear of change
>> as we find ways of welcoming those unwelcomed by many.
We pray especially for... .

Your kingdom come, your will be done
on earth, as in heaven.

We pray, finally, for ourselves.
>> May we become those with the imagination
>> to see the world differently.

May we become those whose sense of our own value has been transformed.
>> May we become those who are no longer paralysed
>>> by the scale of the problems before us,
>> may we be no longer diminished
>>> by our sense of our own smallness.

May our lives be transformed
>> by the kingdom taking root in and through us.
May we become those who take our place and play our part
>> in the transformation and salvation of the world.

Your kingdom come, your will be done
on earth, as in heaven.

Amen.

For the nations

> *Inspired by the feeding of the 5,000 in John 6.1-21*
> *and the hymn 'Guide Me, O Thou Great Redeemer'*

Lord Jesus Christ, Bread of Heaven,
    we pray for our hungry, hurting world.
From today's news, we especially pray for …

We also pray for those countries represented here today.

Lord Jesus Christ, Bread of Heaven,
    whist we rejoice in the goodness of your world,
    with all its diversity and difference,
we also recognise that there are places and situations
    where hell has come to the earth
    and people have become enslaved to the power of death.

Lord Jesus Christ, Bread of Heaven,
    we pray that you will miraculously magnify our own small efforts,
and will turn the gifts of humble fish and loaves that we bring
    into the great feast of your dawning kingdom
    of justice and joy and peace for all.

Lord Jesus Christ, Bread of Heaven,
    we also pray for ourselves.

Forgive us for those times
    when we seek to implement your kingdom on our own terms,
    in our own strength, and sustained by our own resources.

May we instead by those who humbly receive the bread of heaven
    that sustains us for the struggle and nourishes for the task ahead,
when we are called to enter the unsafe, untameable, unbearable territory
    of illness, redundancy, bereavement, danger,
        loss, upheaval, fear, and pressure.

Lord Jesus Christ, Bread of Heaven,
    nourish us to face the future with courage
        and assurance that to the last we are held safe
    and sustained daily by the one who can achieve immeasurably more
        than all we can ask or imagine,
    and who will, at the last, lead us safe to the eternal throne
        and who witnesses to us of the gospel of life,
of the death of death and of the destruction of hells on earth.

Amen.

For society

Inspired by Hebrews 11.32-40

Faithful God, in faith we pray for your world,
    in faith we commit ourselves to the better future
    of your coming kingdom.

We pray for those who conquer kingdoms (v.33),
    for those who pit themselves
    against the principalities and powers of this world,
dedicating their lives to the establishment of your alternative kingdom
    of justice, peace, and equality for all.

We think of those who campaign for equal rights;
    seeking to conquer the insidious narratives
    of segregation and superiority.

We think of those who campaign for peace;
    seeking to conquer the deceptive ideology
    of violence to end violence.

We think of those who campaign for justice,
    seeking to conquer the treacherous dogma of retributive justice
    with your divine justice of restoration.

Faithful God, in faith we pray for your world,
    in faith we commit ourselves to the better future
    of your coming kingdom.

We pray for those who administer justice and the common good,
    for those who make and obtain promises on behalf of us all (v.33).
We think of those who work within the legal systems of our world,
    and we ask that those entrusted with the task
        of determining the lives of others
    would be granted the gifts of impartiality, honesty, and integrity.

FAITH IN DOUBT

We pray especially for those situations known to us
        where justice is not being done,
and where justice systems are failing the weak and the righteous,
        to the advantage of the powerful and the corrupt.

We think also of our political leaders, both national and local.
        May they discover within themselves the capacity
            to resist the corruptive lures of power,
        and to remain true to their calling as servants of the people.
May they choose wisely, listen carefully, and act responsibly.

Faithful God, in faith we pray for your world,
        in faith we commit ourselves to the better future
        of your coming kingdom.

We pray for those who close the mouths of lions and quench raging fires,
        for those who face danger in the cause of right,
        and do battle with the forces of evil in our world (vv.33-34).

We think of those who are active in working to establish peace,
        and whose calling to confront violence
        leads them to places of personal danger.

We think of those who walk alongside the downtrodden,
        the threatened, and the marginalised.

And we pray for those who refuse to devalue
        those whom others have declared valueless,
        standing in solidarity with those facing danger and death.

May they be granted courage and audacity,
        as they call the roaring voices of violence to account,
and quench the fires of ferocity
        with the living water that comes from you.

Faithful God, in faith we pray for your world,
        in faith we commit ourselves to the better future
        of your coming kingdom.

FAITH IN DOUBT

We pray for any who face a martyr's death (vv.35-37).

May they receive the assurance of eternity and the promise of resurrection.
> May they discover the gospel truth
>> that death does not have the final word on life,
> and that suffering and fear are not eternal powers.

May the voices of the martyrs continue to cry out from the ground,
> as the truth of their witness endures undiminished and un-silenced.

Faithful God, in faith we pray for your world,
> in faith we commit ourselves to the better future
> of your coming kingdom.

We pray for those who wander the world
> in poverty and homelessness (v.38)

We think of those who live as refugees,
> of those who have become displaced peoples,
> making lives apart from security and stability.

May their wandering end, and may their children know peace.

We think also of those in our own city who live without homes.
> We pray that they might know the living presence
> of the son of man who had nowhere to lay his head.

We pray for the agencies
> that work to provide people with stable living conditions,
> both in this country and abroad.

Faithful God, in faith we pray for your world,
> in faith we commit ourselves to the better future
> of your coming kingdom.

All these our prayers, we offer in the name of Christ,
> who calls us in faith to live and work
> for the coming kingdom.

Amen.

For love, justice & truth

Inspired by Matthew 5.21-37

Ever-loving and ever-living God,
    we come now to pray in love
    for the life of your world.

Lord of love, we pray for all those
    whose lives are not lived in love.

We pray for those in relationships
    where love has diminished.
We pray for those who have been betrayed by those they love
    and for those who have turned away
    from a love once cherished.

We pray for those who love objects more than people,
    and for those who can only love people
    when they see them as objects.

We pray for those whose actions towards others are not loving,
    and for ourselves when we have not loved others
    as you have loved us.

We thank you that your love is eternal and unending,
    and that you draw the world to you in love.

Lord of justice, we pray for those
    whose lives lack the experience of justice.
We pray for those who are wrongfully imprisoned
    and for those who have been victims
    of injustice within the legal system.

We pray for those who have pursued paths of vengeance and not justice,
    seeking relief for their suffering through the suffering of another.

We pray for those who work to ensure justice is done,
    those who blamelessly uphold the law for the good of all.
We pray for those who mediate between people,
    and who see restoration as the goal of justice.

FAITH IN DOUBT

We thank you that your justice is righteous and loving,
    and that you desire mercy for others,
    as you have mercy on us all.

Lord of integrity, we pray for those
    whose lives are lacking in integrity,
for those who do not speak truth, either to themselves or to others,
    and for those who live as victims of the deceit of others.

We pray also for those who seek to speak truth
    but who face opposition and hostility for their honesty.
May we have the courage to speak truth to power,
    and the wisdom to discern the truth when it is revealed.

We thank you that your truth transcends our capacity for deception,
    and that you challenge us to live lives of integrity and integration.

So, in love, and longing for justice, and committed to integrity,
    we pray now for the current needs of our world…

We commit to your justice,
    all those who live with a tangible experience of injustice,
May those who live with injustice be saved from the path
    of seeking violent retribution against others.

We commit to your truth all those whose lives are lived in deceit,
    and we think especially of those who have been lied to
        and brought to our country on the promise of a better life,
    only to find that they are used and abused
        by those more powerful than they.

God of love, God of justice, God of all truth,
    hear our prayers,
    for the sake of Christ Jesus.

Amen.

For the legal system

Inspired by Matt 5.16-20

Loving God, we come before you now to pray for your world,
    and we lift before you all those who take responsibility for the law.

Lord, in your mercy,
Hear our prayer.

We pray first for those who make the law.

For those who have to take decisions which set precedent,
    for those who advise on legislation,
    and for those who vote laws into being.

We rejoice that, at its best,
    the law reflects the order of creation,
bringing into being communities where the divine gifts
    of freedom, justice, and righteousness
    are enshrined and protected for all.

May our politicians and legal professionals be wise in their decisions,
    and compassionate in their actions.

May they be ever attentive to the vulnerable and marginalised,
    and may they have the courage to resist
    the clamour of the loudest and most powerful voices.

Lord, in your mercy,
Hear our prayer.

We pray for those who dedicate their lives
    to the process of ensuring freedom and justice
    for those affected by the legal processes of our land.

We think of those who bring prosecution,
    seeking justice for victims and vindication for the violated.
We also remember those who seek to defend,
    striving to ensure that the innocent are not found guilty.

And in the midst of this process
>	we recognise the complexities of prosecution and defence,
we recognise the pressures to act in ways
>	that result in the guilty going free
>	or the victim remaining unrepresented.

We thank you for those who take on cases that others will not touch,
>	for those who give their expertise freely or at little cost
>	to help those whom no-one else will stand up for.

We pray for our solicitors, our lawyers, and our judges.
>	Grant them wisdom and integrity,
that the laws they uphold
>	may reflect your greater law of love and righteousness.

Lord, in your mercy,
Hear our prayer.

We pray also for those who enforce the law.
>	For the police, and other law enforcement agencies.

We thank you for those who put themselves at the front line
>	of protecting the weak, defending the victims of crime,
>	and keeping public order, often at great personal cost.

We pray that they may use the powers at their disposal well,
>	and that they may be ever alert to the temptation
>	to act in ways that are partisan or unjust.

May they know the value that you place on each human being,
>	and in the midst of the pressure to objectify the other,
>	may they be guided into paths of righteousness.

Lord, in your mercy,
Hear our prayer.

FAITH IN DOUBT

Finally we pray for those who challenge unjust laws.

We think of those who find
        that their commitment to the path
                of the peaceful kingdom of God
      leads them into conflict
              with the established and enshrined powers that be.

May they know courage, may they be grated discernment,
        and may they see right prevail.

We pray especially for those
        who have become victims of unjust legal processes,
        both in this country and overseas.

We remember those who have been wrongly imprisoned,
        those who have been arrested on false charges,
        and those who face a martyr's death.
May they know that theirs is the kingdom of heaven.

Lord, in your mercy,
Hear our prayer.

Amen.

For the mission of the Spirit

Inspired by the Nazareth Manifesto in Luke 4.16-21

Gracious Spirit of God, your presence ranges far and wide,
    and your loving embrace extends
        to all peoples, and all places, and through all times.

So help us enlarge our own participation
    in the mission to which we have been called.
May we find within ourselves a unity of spirit and purpose
    with the whole great communion of saints.

And so we pray, in solidarity with
    the great and the good,
    and the least and the lost,
        for the world to which we have been sent.
May we be faithful messengers of gospel,
    may we be good news to a hurting and lost world.

Strengthen us for this task,
    and anoint us for our part in the great commission.
Breathe through us the breath of new life for all peoples.

Gentle, gracious Spirit of Christ,
    we look to you for guidance, and we look to you for strength.

We ask you to come upon us,
    and lead and empower us in our lives.
May we be anointed by your presence within us,
    that in all we say and think and do,
        we might live out the mission for which you have been sent:

May we be anointed as those who bring good news to the oppressed.

It is an insult to all creation
        when one human being binds another in oppression,
it is an affront to the kingdom of God
        when power structures are so constructed
        that they promote inequality.

Help us as the Spirit-filled people of God
        to be those who see the value of each human life,
help us to find ways of disrupting oppressive powers
        and restoring divine balance.

May we be anointed as those who bind up the broken-hearted.

All creation suffers when one human being is destroyed
        through grief in their inner being.
The kingdom of God is assailed
        when innocence and joy are ripped away.
The brokenness of inexplicable loss
        is a burden too great for many to bear.

Help us as the Spirit-filled people of God
        to be those who stand alongside those
        whose hearts have been broken,
help us to face the darkness in unity with those who live in darkness,
        and into that darkness to bring a glimmer of light.

May we be anointed as those who proclaim liberty to the captives.

All around us there are those who are held prisoner
        – some as a result of their own actions,
        others as a result of the actions of others.
Some are physically incarcerated,
        others are imprisoned by the torment
        of their own minds and souls.

Help us as the Spirit-filled people of God
        to be those who see restoration where others see vengeance.
Help us to be those who see freedom as the goal of every human soul.

Help us to not turn away from those
        who are hidden from us behind bars and walls.

May we be anointed as those who proclaim the year of Lord's favour.

Year on year we see humanity oppressed,
        broken-hearted and enslaved.
Help us as the Spirit-filled people of God
        to share in the mission of the Spirit
        to see the world changed in the name of Christ Jesus.

Amen.

FAITH IN DOUBT

For when we cannot fix things ourselves

Inspired by the story of Simon Magus in Acts 8.9–24

Gracious God of all good gifts,
    we come before you today
        with the weight of the world in our hearts,
    and with hands empty of solutions.

We cannot solve even the problems of our own lives,
    let alone those facing others,
and we recognise that there is nothing we can put in
    with any guarantee of return.

The world is beyond our control.

Neither can we direct you to attend to our needs and concerns.
    There is no formula of prayer
        that will unlock the powers of heaven
to resolve injustice and vindicate the righteous.

And yet still we come to prayer,
    and we bring before you the needs of the world
        and the concerns of our hearts,
    because we have faith that you are love,
        and that you graciously hear us,
    and that you meet us, and our world, in all our powerlessness;
        to redeem the past and to open the door
        to an alternative future.

We live in uncertain times,
    and there are many voices
        claiming they know the right thing to do,
    and so we pray for our leaders.

Many promises have been made,
    and many more will be made.

The transactional promise that
    'if you vote for me I'll give you what you want'
        underlies so much of our current political discourse.
Help us not to buy into this ideology of giving-to-receive.

FAITH IN DOUBT

And may our politicians, of whatever political persuasion,
> rediscover the integrity of leadership that is needed
> > to govern fairly and for the common good.

We lift our voices against racism, sexism, class war, and homophobia;
> and we commit ourselves to the creation of communities
> > where people are welcomed and valued as individuals
> > rather than as commodities to be traded or manipulated.

So we pray for refugees and asylum seekers.

The statistics speak of the scale of the problem
> but they belie the truth of fathers, mothers, sons, and daughters,
> living lives of uncertainty in camps on our borders,
> or struggling to exist
> > as an invisible segment within our own society.

We pray for those awaiting the processing of asylum claims,
> and we pray for those who cannot see a hopeful future
> for themselves and their families.

We lift our voices against exclusion, protectionism, and selfish politics;
> and we commit ourselves to the creation
> > of hospitable communities of welcome
> where statistics become people, and people become friends.

May we be open to creating a world
> where others are granted opportunities of grace,
to receive freely from you t
> he redemption of the past and hope for the future.

And so we turn our prayers to the deep systems of transaction
> that underlie the inequality of our world.

We name the economic injustices
> that create and perpetuate an imbalance of living
> on both local and global scales.

We pray for those entrusted with the handling of money,
> for bankers and policy makers,
> for financiers and taxation experts.

FAITH IN DOUBT

We lift our voices against injustice, poverty, and extortion;
    and we commit ourselves to the creation
        of communities of equality,
    where money is held lightly,
        and the economics of your coming kingdom
        are made real in our midst
    as we reject any notion of giving-to-receive,
        instead embracing your invitation to give
        with no expectation of reward.

Gracious God of all good gifts,
    we come before you with open hands,
    and we offer to you the gift of our lives.

And we do this because, in faith,
    we believe that you reach out to us in love
to redeem the past and to open the door to a hopeful future.

Amen.

FAITH IN DOUBT

For the stony, thorny, fertile ground of the world

Inspired by the parable of the sower in Mark 4.1–20

Great God of generosity and grace,
    we come now to pray for our world;
to which you have called us, and for which you have given yourself.

We pray for the stony ground of our world,
    for those places where it is hard to live,
    and difficult for any good to survive.

So we think of those who live, year on year, with failed harvests.

For those who do not find on the earth the good news
    of fertile ground and abundant produce.

We think of those who eke out a subsistence
    only to have it taken from them by powerful people
    who already have more than enough but still want more.

We think of those whose farm land is no longer their own,
    and who now till as tenants, growing crops they will never eat,
    and for which they will not receive fair recompense.

We think of those who walk the concrete ground
    of our own towns and cities,
    unsure where their next mean will come from.

So we pray, Great God of generosity and grace,
    for a just and equal sharing of the resources of our world.

From the international policies of the *IMF* and the *World Bank*,
    to the local Food Bank,
    to the care offered by charities and churches,
we pray for all those who speak out in your name against injustice,
    and who seek to model in and through their lives and communities
    the grace and generosity towards others that comes from you.

FAITH IN DOUBT

Great God of generosity and grace,
> we pray for the ground of our world where thorns and weeds grow
> and choke and stifle the seeds of hope and good news.

We think of those whose lives are determined
> by war, fear, and oppressive ideologies.

We think of the young people who grow up knowing that they hate others,
> because all they have experienced from the other
> are acts of hatred towards them.

We recognise the destructive, unending spirals of violence and retribution,
> where good news is subsumed
> beneath systems of protectionism and hatred.

So we pray, Great God of generosity and grace,
> for all those trapped in such systems,
and we long that the seeds of common humanity,
> planted deep within the soul of each person,
will find the space and the grace to take root and grow,
> that the world may be transformed
> as hearts and minds are changed from within.

We pray especially for those who go into the midst of the thorns,
> at risk to themselves, to clear ground for good news to take root.

And finally we pray for ourselves,
> for the fertile ground of our own hearts and minds.

We ask that in our lives, by our words,
> and through our deeds, your kingdom will grow.

We commit ourselves once again to the calling that rests on each of us
> to be agents of good news, activists of transformation,
> and faithful witnesses to the one who has called us:
>> to Jesus Christ, who gave his life
>> for our forgiveness and freedom.

So we pray, Great God of generosity and grace,
> that we may reflect in our life together
> the gracious generosity of your kingdom,
as we share our resources,
> hold lightly to that which we call our own,
> and offer back to you all that we have, and all that we are.

All this we pray, in the name of Jesus our saviour.

Amen.

For a divided world

Inspired by the Sheep and Goats in Matthew 25:31-46

Great God of all the Earth,
> we recognise with sorrow and repentance in our hearts
that all too easily we, your created people,
> rush to the judgement of others.

We divide humanity one from another,
> condemning some and vindicating others.
And always placing ourselves on the side of the righteous.

We isolate those who do not look, live, or love like we do;
> and we put them apart,
telling ourselves that we are right, because they are wrong.

But we hear from your word that in this,
> we bring judgement on ourselves,
every bit as much as we would heap judgement
> on those we would condemn.

Forgive us, dear Lord.

May we instead learn to see others as you see them,
> rather than as we have learned to see them.
May we be given the insight of your Spirit to see through difference
> to discover the common humanity
> > that underlies all our interactions, all our relationships.

And so we pray today for a world
> that seems intent on tearing itself apart.

We look around us at your world,
> and we see so much strife, division, war, suffering, and pain.
We see people rushing to judgment of the other
> and calling down the fires of hell
> > on those who are not like them.

FAITH IN DOUBT

From the breakup of countries and unions,
    to the hatred of one religious group for another,
to the scapegoating of the weak and the vulnerable
    at every level of our society,
we see humans intent on dividing one from another,
    in the interests of naming some as right and some as wrong.

So we pray, today, for the victims of terrorism.

We hold before you all those who will live the rest of their lives
    with the pain and horror.
We pray for those who will have been turned from peace to violence
    by the horror visited upon them.

We pray also for those who work, at great cost to themselves,
    to build bridges between divided peoples.

And we pray also for those who build bridges
    between Islam and Christianity.

We recognise that so much of the violence that we face in our time
    comes from people who claim to be acting
    in obedience to divine command.
And we ask that people of violent faith
    will hear the still small voice of calm
in the midst of their rush to righteous condemnation of the other.

We pray for the persecuted church,
    and for any who face a martyr's death.
May peace and justice prevail
    as your kingdom comes on earth, as in heaven.

We pray for victims of racism in our city of London,
    for those who are marginalised, bullied, and attacked
    because of their ethnicity;
and we pray for asylum seekers, refugees,
    and all those who are denied the possibility of fullness of life
    because of who they are.

May we, as your people in this city, be catalysts of inclusion,
    as we live out our conviction
    that all people are created in your image.

Help us to set aside whatever privilege we have inherited,
> and to be willing to meet the other as equal,
> > whoever they may be.

We pray for all those who find themselves victimised or excluded
> because of their minority sexuality.

We pray especially for those who have been isolated
> from communities of faith,
and whose experience of your body
> has been divisive rather than inclusive.

We thank you for those who are willing to speak out,
> and for those who are willing to reach out
> > and embrace difference.

We pray for the homeless and the vulnerable,
> for those whose economic and personal circumstances
> > give rise to precarious living.

And we name before you the work of our partners and activities
> who seek to bring support and progression
> > to those who feel trapped by life.
We think particularly of …

And so we pray for our church in all its glorious diversity.

We ask that this place will be a beacon of light, love, and inclusion,
> where we discover together that within the love of Christ,
> > all other barriers that would divide are rendered irrelevant.

We pray that all will be welcome here,
> regardless of ethnicity, social standing, gender, or sexuality.

And that we will have the courage
> to live the truth of your glorious gospel of unity
> > in the midst of our divided city.

Amen.

For integrity in intercession

Inspired by Lamentations 2

Loving God whose embrace enfolds all pain, suffering, loss, and grief;
    we come to you today with hearts heavy at the state of the world.

From the local and personalized traumas
    of our own lives and those whom we love,
to the national and international scandals
    of inequality, injustice, and political violence.

From terrorism to 'just warfare',
    we assert that whenever one human
        takes physical action against another,
    we are very far from your kingdom of justice and peace.

So forgive us when we cry 'peace, peace' when there is no peace.

Forgive us when we turn away, turn off,
    and ignore the suffering of others
whether it is on our own doorstep, in our own community,
    or on the other side of the world.

Give us a renewed commitment
    to the humanity we hold in common with others,
and a renewed insight into the darkness t
    hat lurks in our own souls also.

May we never be complacent enough
    to think that it could never happen here,
    that it could never happen to me,
    that *we* could never do *that* to another.

Rather, may we be ever alert to the evil
    that prowls our world seeking agency to act,
whispering lies into human hearts,
    and setting one against another.

May sin be exposed to the light of truth,
    not painted over or hidden from view.

FAITH IN DOUBT

So we pray now for our city:
> the beautiful, joyful, prosperous,
> compelling city of London.

We express before you our love for and commitment to
> this diverse conglomeration of humanity,

and because of this we turn our thoughts
> to those who suffer in our midst.

We pray for those who do not have enough money to make ends meet,
> those on benefits or working multiple low-paid jobs.

We think of those who have to choose between heating and food,
> because they cannot afford both;

and of those who are indebted to lenders
> who threaten and extort to get their interest.

We pray for those who cannot afford housing,
> and who live in overcrowded conditions,
> or in hostels, or on the streets;

and we pray for those who have come here as refugees,
> seeking a new life in a strange new city
> and finding that it is neither easy nor straightforward to do so.

And so we commit to you the efforts of those
> who are seeking to make this city a better place,

and we think particularly of those schools, universities,
> synagogues, mosques, and churches
> which make up the *London Citizens* movement.

May we, together, be able to achieve
> what none of us could do on our own.

But we also lift our prayers beyond the horizon of our own city,
> and we pray for countries torn apart b
> y war and decimated by oppression.

We think of Syria, Iran, Palestine,
> Yemen, Somalia, South Sudan, and Nigeria.

We hear the words of the United Nations Humanitarian Chief,
> that 'we stand at a critical point in history',
and we commit ourselves and our resources
> to the service of your kingdom of justice and peace.

We pray for all those seeking a resolution to war,
> and alleviation of famine.

And in all this, as with so much else that is on our hearts,
> we ask for your peace, courage, and love.

May peace prevail, may we have courage to act,
> and in all things may love triumph.

In the name of Jesus Christ,
> who endured the cross for the sake of the whole world.

Amen.

For the wisdom of waiting

> *Inspired by Jesus writing on the ground with his finger in John 8.8*

Merciful Jesus, we meet you in the long pause,
> the silent moment, the reflective breath.

And in that encounter we confront our own inadequacies,
> and we meet forgiveness.

Help us to learn from you to not rush to judgment.
> Help us to learn the wisdom of waiting before speaking.

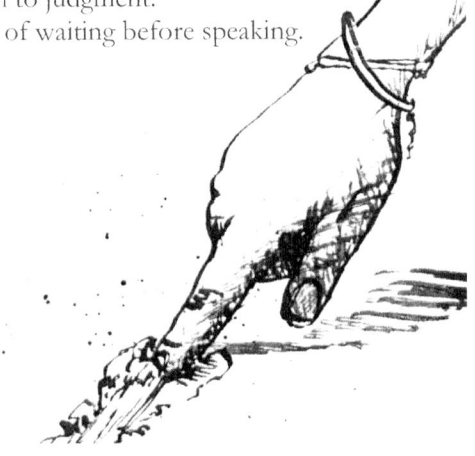

Amen.

For new life, new hope, and new joy

Inspired by the Magnificat in Luke 1.46-55

God of new life, new hope, and new joy,
> we pray now for those people and places
> in whom hope and joy have died.

We pray for those who mourn,
> and ask that you will comfort them.
We pray for those who experience life as oppression and injustice,
> and ask that you will uplift them.
We pray for those who are hungry, homeless, and helpless,
> and ask that they will be fed and housed.
We pray for those who are lonely and isolated,
> and ask that they will know that they are loved.

So we pray for those who work for justice,
> for lawyers and advocates, for campaigners and politicians,
> that they will be given courage to speak, and wisdom to act.

We pray for those who care for the poor and the vulnerable,
> that their efforts will lead to lasting change in the lives of others.

We pray for those who reach out across barriers that divide,
> bringing companionship and acceptance
> to those who find themselves cut off from others.

And we pray for ourselves,
> as we too seek to play our part in your coming kingdom.
May we be those who see hope where others see despair,
> life where others see death,
and so may we proclaim and live into being
> the good news of Jesus Christ.

Amen.

For the signs of the coming kingdom

Inspired by the Wedding at Cana in John 2.1-11

Loving God of abundant grace,
        as we bring our prayers to you today
we offer our gratitude and thanksgiving
        for the good things in our lives,
for those times and places and people
        who bring us joy and happiness.

We thank you for these signs of your coming kingdom.

We also offer to you those areas of our lives
        which have yet to experience the transformation of your presence:
the hidden shame, the unacknowledged addictions,
        the broken relationships.

We ask that you will bring healing, forgiveness, and new life into our lives,
        that we may more fully live in the light of your love
            as revealed in Christ Jesus.

So we pray now for all those known to us
        who live lives of unfulfilled hope,
            for those who contemplate the future with fear or despair.
We ask that, like the guests at the wedding in Cana of Galilee,
        they will discover through your presence
            an unexpected gift of grace.

May those who mourn be comforted,
        may those who are put-upon find help,
may those who hunger and thirst be satisfied,
        may those who are fearful find solace,
may those who doubt be reassured,
        may those who are discouraged find courage,
may those who are shamed be honoured,
        may those who are sinful find forgiveness.

FAITH IN DOUBT

In a moment of silence now,
> we hold before you those situations
> that you have placed on our hearts.

May the presence of Christ who turns water into wine,
> be present to our lives and our world,
surprising us with new hope, new life, and new joy,
> revealing the coming kingdom of justice and peace,
> for which we long and pray.

Amen.

For enquiring minds

Inspired by Doubting Thomas in John 20.24-29

Great God of all love,
    we come today to pray for those who seek after truth,
        for those who seek after knowledge,
    for those who will not be silenced by ideology or dogma,
        but will continue to ask the difficult questions
        even when others would rather they didn't.

So we pray for scientists and engineers,
    in their quest for evidence
    and their desire to understand the world.
We thank you that we live in an ordered world,
    where energy can be harnessed for good
    and knowledge can transform our engagement with creation.

We pray for all those who seek to think your thoughts after you,
    to understand the complexities of creation;
    and we rejoice in their triumphs.

We thank you for those scientists
    who have spoken so clearly and courageously
    on the issue of climate change,
issuing their warnings despite the huge pressure on them
    to remain silent.

We thank you for those engineers
    who are finding solutions to global problems,
and are seeking to find new ways
    to harness energy for the good of all.

We pray also for those
> who have to take difficult ethical decisions in their work.
May they be guided by you in the application of their efforts,
> that the world may be transformed for good.

We pray for those in the medical profession,
> who have to deal on a daily basis
> > with the difficult truths of life and death.

We pray for those who offer care when life is fading,
> and for those who through the application of their skill
> > bring life back into being when it would otherwise have ended.

May they know that they are doing your work,
> as they unflinchingly stare death in the face,
> putting their hands in other people's wounds,
> and seeking after life in all its fullness.

And may they know that death is not the ultimate enemy,
> as its hold over human existence met its end
> > in the resurrection of your son Jesus Christ.

We pray for lawyers, solicitors, judges,
> and all those in the legal profession,
> > whose calling it is to weigh evidence,
> > and to seek after truth.

We thank you that they will keep searching for evidence
> to corroborate the testimony of others.

We thank you for their commitment to justice,
> and for the legal system that provides
> > the framework for their efforts.

We pray for those countries where judges are corrupt,
> where bribery is rife,
> and the application of law is capricious.

We pray for all those wrongfully imprisoned, scapegoated, or targeted,
> may they find in Christ, who was executed for no reason,
> > a source of hope and new life when all hope seems to have passed.

FAITH IN DOUBT

Pass through the locked doors of their prisons,
    breathe your Spirit of peace into their lives,
    and release them from fear.

And lastly we pray for our theologians,
    for those in all religions
    who seek to ask the difficult question of you.

We pray for ministers and vicars, and rabbis and imams,
    we pray for those who study the scriptures with integrity,
    seeking to open people's minds to the greatness of a God of love.

We pray for those who work in the universities of our country,
    researching and teaching the great texts and stories of faith.

May their insights be fruitful for your great kingdom of love,
    and may their quest for truth bring life and faith
    to those who join them in their questioning.

All this we pray in the name of Jesus Christ,

Amen.

WORDS FOR THE LORD'S TABLE

At the Lord's Table we believe that we have the opportunity to meet Christ in a special way: in 'communion' we are gathered with those who are present and also with the wider communion of saints. At the first communion Jesus offered a prayer, and therefore as we gather in memory of him we too offer our prayers of confession, thanksgiving, and intercession.

These prayers have emerged from reflection on the significance of the sharing of bread and wine as a moment of sacramental encounter, where our obedient response to the call of Christ to eat and drink is met with Christ's presence drawing near to us by the Spirit.

For the substance of eternity

Creative God of mystery and history,
> we give you thanks
>> that you reach into the everyday stuff of our lives;
> drawing us beyond the mundane
>> to touch the stuff of eternity.

So we thank you for this bread and this wine,
> this ordinary, everyday food and drink
>> – the stuff of our sustenance;
> and yet in this bread and wine we see the eternal made flesh.

In this bread and wine,
> we encounter the body of your son Jesus Christ,
>> broken for our forgiveness
> and made real in our lives by the action of your Spirit.

May we, as we eat and drink,
> become ever more aware of the substance of eternity,
as we take into ourselves your loving forgiveness and acceptance.

May we be shaped ever more into likeness of your son,
> as we become his body on the earth.

So for this bread and wine we give you thanks.

Amen.

For an end to violence

Great God of love, we have gathered in your presence to meet with you,
and you have met with us at our point of deepest need
    by giving yourself utterly to us.

Living God of the cross,
    where we are scared, you have comforted us,
    where we are weak, you have strengthened us,
where we sorrowful and lonely,
    you have sat alongside us and offered us peace.

And in this encounter with you
    we see your deepest nature revealed.
As we meet you in the body of Christ,
    broken for us and shared among us for our salvation,
we understand more of your great plan
    for the salvation of the world.

You are not a God of war, violence, tribalism, or territorialism,
    and you do not ask your followers
    to march to victory in your name,
nor to establish your kingdom on the earth
    by means of force and coercion.

Rather, you are the God of the cross,
    the God of self-giving love,
    the God who is poured out for others and broken for all.
You are the God who gives, and gives, and gives,
    with no expectation of reward or repayment.

And it is in your name, and as your people,
    that we come now to pay for the needs of your world,
offering ourselves as the answer to our prayers,
    even as we lay them before you.
We are your body, and this is your world.

In all these prayers, we offer ourselves to you,
    for the purposes of building your peaceable kingdom,
    on earth, as it is in heaven.

Amen.

For a peaceful future

Loving God of all creation we give you thanks and praise
> for all your great love which you have shown to us.

Above all we praise you for the new way through violence
> which opened before humanity
> in the crucifixion of your son Jesus Christ.

When we look at the world in which we live,
> we see so often people living with pain and suffering,
> fear and failure, threat and uncertainty.

We pray for all those whose lives are dominated
> by the powers of sin and death.
May your new way to life be true for them,
> as hope and justice displace despair and defeat.

We pray especially this day for all those who live under occupation.

We think of the Palestinians in the occupied territories,
> we think of those in Syria, Iraq, and Lebanon,
> whose homelands have been taken by extremist forces.

For all those whose homes have been taken from them by force,
> we offer our prayers of intercession
> and our willingness to stand in solidarity with their suffering.

We pray especially for all those
> who work to achieve peace and reconciliation.

Great God of new life, we commit ourselves
> to the path of hospitality and inclusion,
and we thank you for the opportunities
> that our own freedom and democracy
> give for us to speak out for others.

FAITH IN DOUBT

As we have shared bread and wine this day,
> we have been reminded of the great feast of your coming kingdom.

And in our own sharing, we catch a glimpse of the great redistribution
> that is part of your vision for a renewed humanity.

Help us to be generous to all,
> and to see your image reflected in each created human soul;

help us to see the spark of divine life in each person,
> and to remember that it was for every person
> that you were prepared to give your all.

May the cross make it true for us, and in our world,
> that the wall that divides us is broken down.

Give us compassionate hearts
> that we might live and work for your coming kingdom,
> that all may be included, and none kept out.

So we name of the divisions that blight humanity,
> divisions of ethnicity, social standing, gender, and sexuality,

and we say before you that we will not live at ease
> while such divisions remain part of our world.

Reach out through us, your people,
> to those whom others would seek to exclude.

May it be true in our lives, and in our life together,
> that your kingdom banquet of welcome and celebration
>> is open to all,
> that all may see how great is the love that you have for them.

We offer these prayers in the name of Christ Jesus our Lord.

Amen.

For a world needing bread and wine

Inspired by the feeding of the 5000

Great God of creative abundance,
    we come before you today
        as a people in need of your generous blessing,
    and so we offer ourselves to you,
        with open hands and receptive hearts.

Take away from us our pretensions of self-reliance,
    and unmask for us our images of self-security.

Help us to realise that our fleeting blessings of health, wealth, and power
    are fragile idols of sustenance,
    and that we entrust our souls to them at our peril.

May we learn instead to see ourselves and our world with your eyes;
    may we come to appreciate where true value lies;
    both within ourselves, and in the lives of others.

May our eyes be opened to the gentle gifts of grace
    that you have placed in our midst,
and may we come to value the abundance
    of your hidden yet dawning kingdom,
    as it is made real amongst us.

And so we offer ourselves to your service:
    take the gifts of our lives, and bless them,
    that we might become a blessing to others.

Whether we bring wealth or weakness,
    power or poverty, health or helplessness;
we place our lives into your hands, and we ask for your blessing.

We offer before you today the resources of this church;
    we offer our resources of people,
        from pastors to volunteers to occasional attendees;
    we offer our resources of money,
        from that which sits in our personal bank accounts
        to that which we hold collectively as a community;

we offer our building, our contacts,
> our friendships, our whole bodies,
and the body of Christ that is this church in this place.

May we learn together the lesson
> that hoarding the resources of the kingdom
> is not what we are called to do.

Grant us the courage to release to your service
> the gifts you have given us.

And so, mindful of the needs of others,
> we pray for those who live in need,
> poverty, uncertainty, and fear;
aware that you call us to play our own part
> in the coming of your kingdom of peace and justice.

We pray for all those who are hungry today,
> and especially for those who have this week
> > used a food bank for the first time
> > in order to feed themselves or their families.

We pray for all those who will share
> with one another today the blessing of food.
May this tangible sign of your kingdom
> be transformative and life-giving in our midst.

As we have shared bread and wine,
> symbols of your body made whole,
we pray for those who have an unhealthy
> or abusive relationship with food and drink.

From the obese to the anorexic,
> from the middle class drinker to the hardened alcoholic.

We recognise how easily the kingdom blessings of food and wine
> can become distorted in our own bodies.

And so we pray for all those who will visit an anonymous group this week.
> May we, each of us, learn to see ourselves as you see us,
> that through our bodies your body may be made known.

We pray for those who have the power to make changes at a national level,
> for policy-makers, politicians, and business and industry leaders.
Keep them from the dehumanising commodification of humanity,
> and may they instead find ways
> > of bringing the body politic to health for the common good.

We ask for, and commit ourselves to, your transformative vision
> of a just and equal society, where none go hungry and all are fed.

And so, finally, we pray for ourselves.

May we learn to share
> both the hidden and visible blessings of our lives,
offering ourselves and all that we are and have,
> to the service of your in-breaking kingdom of equality and justice.

In the name of Jesus Christ,

Amen.

For Communion in Advent

*Advent*urous God, we marvel at the ways in which you come to us,
    through the courage of the prophets,
        through the faithfulness of the priests,
    through the openness of women and men to new life,
        through vulnerability and fragility,
    through water, bread, and wine.

And so we pray for a world
    that is ever needful of your coming.

We pray for those who have no voice,
    for those who pass silently through our world,
        ignored and side-lined, marginalised and dispossessed.
We think of those in our society who are homeless,
    of those who live with disability,
        of those who are refugees and cannot speak English;
and we give thanks for those who can speak out,
    for those who advocate,
        and for those who seek to empower others.

We pray for those who have no voice.

We pray also for those who struggle with faith,
    for whom doubt is crippling,
        who long to see you, but just can't find you.

We offer our thanks for the rituals of faith
    that keep the rumour of your coming alive.
May those who seek, find,
    and may those who are lost, be found.
We pray for those who struggle with faith.

We pray also for all new parents,
> as through each fragile new life, made in your image,
> you commit yourself once again to this world.

We thank you for the examples of Zechariah and Elizabeth,
> and Mary and Joseph, and Abraham and Sarah.

Be with those who long for children but cannot conceive,
> and with those whose children are unplanned,
> and with those children who are fighting for life.

In the midst of the complexities of our lives,
> come to us afresh to spark hope, joy, and life.

We pray for all new parents.

We pray for ourselves,
> and we open our own lives to your coming,
>> as you re-shape us, and re-make us,
>> and forgive us, and renew us.

May we know you deeply,
> and have the courage to speak,
> the faith to persevere,
> the vulnerability to risk,
> and the hope to seek after your coming.

All these prayers we offer through our saviour Jesus Christ,
> God made flesh.

Amen.

For Easter Day communion

Words of institution (responsive)

We are the body of Christ.
And we come today to break bread
    and to pour out wine in memory of him.

The body of Christ is broken for us,
    We are broken.
    I am broken, you are broken.
    We have broken the body of Christ

The blood of Christ is poured out for our transgressions.
    We are full of sin.
    I am sinful, you are sinful.
    And it is only by his wounds that we are healed.

The body of Christ is raised for our forgiveness.
    We are broken and sinful.
And yet we are healed.
    I am forgiven, you are forgiven.
    We are forgiven

The body of Christ eternally bears the marks of crucifixion.
And we return to this table to repeat the story
    of brokenness and healing, of sin and forgiveness.
Because we still sin, and we are still broken.

Christ is risen.
He is risen indeed.

So let us eat bread, drink wine,
    and take deep within ourselves the reality of the cross,
that on this day of new life,
    we might find healing, forgiveness, and resurrection.

Prayer of Thanksgiving for the Bread and Wine

Great God of all time and all places,
We offer you our thanks and praise for the gift of this day,
    for the gift of one another gathered around this table,
    for the gift of new life,
        for the gift of our bodies,
            for the gift of food and drink.

As the disciples met you on the road to Emmaus,
    and recognised you in the sharing of bread and wine,
may we discover you alongside us,
    and recognise your presence with us.

We thank you especially for these gifts of bread and wine,
    given to bring us strength and joy.
May we be made strong in your life and love,
    and may we be joyful in our living and loving.

Amen.

For online communion: Scattered yet Gathered

A liturgy in two voices for sharing communion whilst scattered.

Jesus said:
'Very truly, I tell you, whoever believes has eternal life.
I am the bread of life.
Your ancestors ate the manna in the wilderness, and they died.
This is the bread that comes down from heaven,
so that one may eat of it and not die.
I am the living bread that came down from heaven.
Whoever eats of this bread will live forever;
and the bread that I will give for the life of the world is my flesh.'
(John 6.47-51)

We are the people of God,
we are the body of Christ.
We are scattered, and the body of Christ is broken,
but as we gather, the body of Christ is re-membered.

So together we gather in obedience to Jesus' command,
to remember, and to share together
> **in breaking bread and drinking wine,**
in remembrance of the death of Christ.

Each piece of bread that we eat
> **was once scattered across the fields,**

> and the grain that God gave to grow
> has become for us the bread of life.

Each sip of wine that we drink was once many vines,
> and the grapes that God gave to grow
> have become for us the new wine of God's kingdom.

In our communion with one another,
> we are fed with the bread of heaven that sustains us,
> **and we drink the wine of gladness that brings us joy.**

**The people of Israel were sustained by God
through their years of wilderness wandering:**

'The Israelites ate manna forty years,
>until they came to a habitable land;
they ate manna, until they came
>to the border of the land of Canaan.'
(Exodus 16.35)

**'[God] rained down on them manna to eat,
>and gave them the grain of heaven.'
(Psalm 78.24)**

And we too are God's people,
>sustained by God through the wilderness of this world.

**Jesus said to his disciples:
'Our ancestors ate the manna in the wilderness;
as it is written, 'He gave them bread from heaven to eat.'**

Then Jesus said to them,
"Very truly, I tell you,
>it was not Moses who gave you the bread from heaven,
>but it is my Father who gives you the true bread from heaven.
For the bread of God is that which comes down from heaven
>and gives life to the world."

They said to him, "Sir, give us this bread always."
Jesus said to them, "I am the bread of life.
>Whoever comes to me will never be hungry,
>and whoever believes in me will never be thirsty."'
(John 6.31-35)

**On the night on which Jesus was betrayed,
>he sat at supper with his disciples.
While they were eating, he took a piece of bread,
>said a blessing broke it, and gave it to them with the words,**
'This is my body. It is for you. Do this to remember me.'

Later, he took a cup of wine, saying,
'This cup is God's new covenant, sealed with my blood.
    Drink from it, all of you, to remember me'.

So now, following Jesus' example and command,
    we take this bread and this wine,
the ordinary things of the world
    which Christ will make special.
And as he said a prayer before sharing, let us do so, too

God of all those who are scattered and broken,
    you call us to wholeness.
We thank you for the love demonstrated in giving your son,
    that we might be united with you.
We thank you that in Christ you enter into
    the pain, uncertainty, and fear of our world;
and that your arms are open in loving embrace,
    gathering us to you as a mother hen
    gathers her brood under her wing,
as a shepherd gathers his flock.

We thank you for bread and wine,
    symbols and signs for us today
of your faithfulness to your people through all generations.

Amen.

'Hear the word of the LORD, O nations,
>   and declare it in the coastlands far away;
say, "He who scattered Israel will gather him,
>   and will keep him as a shepherd a flock."'
(Jeremiah 31.10)

Let us share in bread together.

'Then all the Judeans returned
>   from all the places to which they had been scattered
and came to the land of Judah, to Gedaliah at Mizpah;
>   and they gathered wine and summer fruits in great abundance.
(Jeremiah 40.12).

Let us share in wine together.

Jesus said
'The hour is coming, indeed it has come,
>   when you will be scattered, each one to his home,
>   and you will leave me alone.
Yet I am not alone because the Father is with me.
I have said this to you, so that in me you may have peace.
>   In the world you face persecution.
But take courage; I have conquered the world!"'
(John 16.32-33)

WORDS FOR TIMES AND SEASONS

The liturgical year and the lectionaries that support it can help us root our faith in the rhythm of life. We find ourselves inhabiting them as we live out the months and years our own lives. There is a sense of movement, from Advent to Christmas, from Lent to Easter to Pentecost… as each year we journey again through the stories that define our faith.

At Bloomsbury we have tended to use a lectionary to guide us in our journey through the Christian year. For many years it was the Revised Common Lectionary, but more recently we have found the Narrative Lectionary to be helpful.

In these prayers, I have tried to reflect on particular turning-points in the year, particularly where the rhythm of the church's worship coincides with a sense of our mortality before God.

For Good Friday

God of the cross, we gather today
>>with the great multitude of disciples across time and space,
>>to look up into the face of our crucified messiah.
Today is the day when we confront death in all its stark reality,
>>recognising that where you have already gone,
>>we too will one day follow.

Jesus, remember us, when you come into your kingdom.

We remember all those who today face the reality of death.
>>We commit to your loving care
>>>those who are nearing the end of their lives
>>>through age, illness, and infirmity,
>>and we particularly think of those known to us
>>>who are drawing near to the end.

Be with them we pray,
>>and may they know the comfort
>>of your eternal love which transcends death.

Jesus, remember us, when you come into your kingdom.

We remember all those who live in constant fear for their lives,
>>for those whose daily routine
>>>includes bombs and guns, intimidation and terror.

We pray for those for whom life is cheap,
>>and for those for whom the cost of survival is too high.

Be with those for whom life is uncertain,
>>and be present to those who do not know if they can carry on.
May they know the comfort of your eternal love which transcends death.

We give thanks for those who bring healing and peace
>>to a world of darkness,
and for those who offer hope to the hopeless.

Jesus, remember us, when you come into your kingdom.

We remember those who mourn,
> who live daily with the pain of loss,
and we pray for those whose loved ones are dying,
> for those who care for partners with terminal illness,
> and for those living with dementia.

May they find comfort in the security
> of your eternal love which transcends death.

God of the cross, we offer you our prayers
> in the certain knowledge of your great love.

Jesus, remember us, when you come into your kingdom.

Amen.

For Easter Day and Resurrection Hope.

Lord Jesus Christ, giver of new life,
> bringer of resurrection hope,
we pray for a world where death is dominant,
> and finality is feared.

We pray for those known to us
> who are struggling to live with a diagnosis of terminal illness,
> either for themselves or for someone dear to them.

We pray that each day will be a gift of grace,
> and that in the midst of pain and sorrow
>> will be found moments of goodness
> that point to your steadfast and unfailing love
>> which casts out all fear.

Lord of new life, hear our prayers for resurrection.

We pray for those who have been victimised
> by war and terrorist outrage.
> We remember before you especially …
We pray for peace, and for reconciliation
> between peoples who struggle to relate in ways
> other than through the lens of death.

May those who see the death of others
> as the solution to problems
be granted a glimpse of the precious gift of life
> which you gift to each human soul.
May those who live in fear of death at the hands of others
> find courage and peace and release from their fears.

Lord of new life, hear our prayers for resurrection.

We pray for those who are victims of natural disasters.
>   We remember…

We remember also those who are facing the impact of climate change,
>   those whose land is not the same as it used to be,
>   and who now struggle to survive in the face of increased flooding,
>   or unpredictable weather patterns.

Lord of all creation, we join our voices with the groaning of our planet,
>   and we pray for those who work to bring life
>   to those who live in difficult and dangerous places.

Lord of new life, hear our prayers for resurrection.

We pray for those who transform communities.
>   Those whose lives tell stories of resurrection
>   in the midst of the ordinary.

We give thanks for those who live lives of love, justice,
>   reconciliation, and care for others.
We pray for those who live the values
>   of your dawning kingdom of new life for all,
and we commit ourselves anew
>   to your service that together we might show ourselves
>   ready to live according to your will.

Lord of new life, hear our prayers for resurrection.

And finally, we pray for ourselves.
> We own before you our fears for our own lives,
>> the inevitability of our own mortality.
We confess the many deaths that blight our days;
> deaths of hope, ambition, love, compassion and desire.

Grant us today the gift of renewed life.
> Restore us to life, and bring us to fullness in you.
May our lives become gifts of resurrection to others,
> may new life come through us,
> may our lives make your new life known and real in this world.

Lord Jesus Christ, giver of new life,
> bringer of resurrection hope,
we pray for a world where death is dominant,
> and finality is feared.

And in our praying we proclaim the good news of the gospel of Christ,
> the good news that death is not the final answer to life,
> that the good news of resurrection
> is indeed good news for all people.

Amen.

For Low Sunday, or Quasimodo Sunday

Inspired by 1 Peter 2.1-5: Quasi modo geniti infantes

Like newborn infants, we come to God,
        longing for pure, spiritual milk.
We long to grow into salvation.

Like starving children, we come to God,
        longing to taste that the Lord is Good.
We long to grow into salvation.

Aware of our sin, we come to God,
        longing to be rid of all that keeps us from God.
We long to grow into salvation.

Seeking God, we turn to Christ,
        who builds his holy house with the living stones of our lives.
We long to grow into salvation.

Seeking Christ, we offer ourselves
        as spiritual sacrifices to the God of love.
We long to grow into salvation.

Amen.

For Transfiguration Sunday

Great God of mountaintop and valley-depth
    we gather to seek your presence today.

We come from far and wide,
    from the four corners of our city and beyond;
and as we gather we bring our lives,
    with all their diversity and complexity,
into the your loving, living presence,
    for transformation and healing and renewal.

Some of us have come from happy homes
    and some of us have come from troubled corners.
Some of us come to offer praise and thanksgiving,
    and some of us come to offer pain and distress.
We come from both mountaintop and valley-depth,
    but we have come,
    because you have called us.

God of transfiguration,
    may we today encounter you with unveiled faces.
Keep us from hiding behind the veils
    of self-deception, fear, and inadequacy.

May we today encounter you face-to-face,
    may we learn to see ourselves as you see us,
    and may we learn to see our world as you see it.

May your kingdom come
    as we, your people, meet with you.
May your kingdom come
    as we, your people, are transformed by you.
May your spirit rest with us all.

For the sake of Christ Jesus our saviour.

Amen.

For Mothering Sunday

God of love, mother of us all,
>we give thanks for the life that you have brought to birth in us.

We thank you for the gift of this day,
>and for our own lives, these precious gifts of incarnation.

We pray today for all those who are being brought to life.
>We pray for unborn babies, for expectant parents,
>>for excited and fearful grandparents,
>>for good families and loving relatives.
>
>We pray also for all those whose experience
>>of new life is unexpected,
>>troubling, or traumatic:
>
>We pray for refugees, for victims, and for all those
>>who fear for the health and future of their children.

We recognise in you the mystery of life,
>and your willingness to recommit yourself to your children
>in the midst of all our failings and faults.

Loving God, thank you for your tender care.

God of love, mother of us all,
>we give thanks for your steadfast love for each of us, your children.

We thank you that you never turn your face from us,
>and that your gaze is ever of love and not despair.

We pray for all those who struggle with the responsibilities of childcare,
>for those who find their own deepest fears and doubts
>>reflected back at them in the lives
>>of those whom they have brought into being.

And so we commit to your loving protection
>all those whose parents have failed them,

and we pray for those who seek to provide care and nurturing
>where others have been unable to do so,
>and in so doing echo your own love for each created soul.

So we pray for adopted parents, for step-parents,
> for foster carers, social workers,
>> and all those who work in the juvenile care system.

May they discover in their role,
> the love that you extend through them to those in their care.

Loving God, thank you for your tender care.

God of love, mother of us all,
> we give thanks that you sustain us
>> and support us throughout our lives.

We thank you for our bodies,
> and we thank you for those who care for them
>> helping us keep healthy, and intervening when we face illness.

With each passing year,
> we grow ever more aware of our own mortality,
>> and we are grateful for our own continuing lives.

So we pray today for those who are reaching the end of their lives,
> for those who are very old, and for those who are very ill.

Give comfort and assurance in place of fear and doubt,
> and hold in your eternal embrace
>> all those who long for your loving touch.

We pray for nurses and doctors,
> for hospice workers and hospital chaplains,
>> and for all those who work in healthcare.

And we ask that, when our own lives draw to their conclusion,
> we will know good care and love
>> as we make our own journey into your eternity.

Loving God, thank you for your tender care.

God of love, mother of us all,
> we give thanks for the church which nourishes us,
> and enables us to grow.

We thank you for this body, which is your gathered congregation
> drawn together in this place, and at this time.

We pray for one another,
> with all our diverse needs and cares and joys and sorrows.

May we experience your love for us
> as we discover our mutual love for one another.

As we have shared bread and wine together,
> may we learn ever more clearly what it means
> to participate in your body.

We pray for our new members,
> and rejoice that you have brought them into our midst.

May they bless us with their presence,
> and may we bless them with your loving care.

Help us to discern one another's needs,
> and to be active in carrying one another's burdens.

Loving God, thank you for your tender care.

God of love, mother of us all,
> we give thanks for the gift of those who love us,
> and those whom we love.

We thank you for friends and family,
> and in silence now we name in our hearts before you,
> all those whom we love, and who love us.

\<silence\>

Thank you, loving God for your tender care.

Amen.

For Father's Day

God of all love, forgiveness, and patience,
> we rejoice that you have called us into your presence.

As many today celebrate Father's day,
> and others celebrate Trinity Sunday

so we give thanks for those aspects of your eternal nature
> that we experience as the perfected love of a father to a child.

We thank you for your faithfulness, and your protection,
> and we thank you for your loving embrace,
>> that forgives all our failings.

We pray for all those who are fathers,
> and for those who will be new fathers.

We pray for those who have lost their fathers,
> and for those who have never known their fathers.

We pray for those whose fathers were not all that they should have been,
> and for those who do not know how to father their children.

We rejoice that in the eternal divine movement
> that is one God: Divine Parent,
> Eternal Son, and ever-present Spirit,

we are invited into a relationship
> of love, forgiveness, and patience.

Amen.

For Remembrance Sunday

In the name of Jesus, we will remember
We will remember

Great God of everlasting peace and eternal justice,
>we live in a world where memories are short,
>and history is rewritten.

As one generation gives way to the next,
>the lessons of the past are forgotten,
>and the spirals of violence are allowed to begin once again.

We look around us at the world we live in,
>and we see posturing and protectionism,
>>we see poverty and prosperity,
>>>we see power and propaganda,
>but we do not see peace.

All too easily our world turns to war as the solution to problems,
>and we forget that armed conflict is never a final solution,
>and that war is always counter-productive to the cause of peace.

So in our world of hatred and division we turn to you,
>the great eternal force of love that transcends generations,
>and we ask that you will help us to remember.

Help us to speak truths of peace and justice in our time,
>as we tell your story of forgiveness,
to those who have never heard it,
>and to those who have wilfully forgotten it.

In the name of Jesus, we will remember
We will remember

FAITH IN DOUBT

On this day of remembering, we turn to the cross:
> the great symbol of violence, oppression, and execution
> which lies at the heart of our commitment to peace.

May we rediscover what it means
> to live lives in the light of the cross as the end of violence.

May we rediscover in your story the eternal truth
> that all conflict ultimately ends
> in the victimisation and death of the innocent.

Forgive us when we are tempted to believe
> that 'fighting for peace' is anything other
> than a deception to justify violence.

Help us to find courage to speak into being your alternative story,
> that the only true path to peace
> lies through forgiveness and reconciliation.

And in a world where death so often seems to get the final word,
> we ask that you will awaken us to the hope of resurrection,

where death is itself defeated, and peace and justice are fulfilled.

May we never forget the hope that lies at the heart of your story.

In the name of Jesus, we will remember
We will remember

So with hope set before us, and your eternal perspective behind us,
> we come now to pray for the transformation of our world.

In a world of violence, we dare to speak our conviction
> that it does not have to be this way.

And as we speak into being your alternative world of peace and justice,
> we commit ourselves to living out the truth of that conviction,
> until it is true in our world.

So we pray for all those who, this day, are fighting:
> We pray for all those who will kill another human being in war
>> because they believe that it is the right thing to do.
>
> We pray for those who will kill another in war
>> because they believe that they have no choice.
>
> We pray for those who will kill another
>> because it is the only way they know they are alive.

For all those who will kill, we pray forgiveness and mercy.
> May they discover in their lives the truth spoken from the cross,
> that forgiveness is offered even to those who kill the innocent.

'Father, forgive them, for they know not what they do.'

In the name of Jesus, we will remember
We will remember

We pray for all those who are victims of war:
> We pray for civilians who are killed
>> as they try to live their lives in peace.
>
> We pray for refugees driven from their homes
>> to seek a new life elsewhere.
>
> We pray for wounded soldiers,
>> discharged by the country they fought for
>> and now reliant on charity to build a new life.

For all those who have been victimized by war,
>	may they discover in their lives the solidarity of the cross,
and may they come to know the path
>	to resurrection that lies through death.

'Blessed are those who mourn, for they shall be comforted.'

In the name of Jesus, we will remember
We will remember

We pray for politicians and power-brokers,
>	for peace-makers and peace-keepers.
We pray for prime ministers and presidents;
>	may they remember all those
>	whom they have been elected to represent.
May they remember the lessons of the past,
>	and the price paid by so many
>	in the service of ideologies of violence.
May they come to the conviction that it doesn't have to be this way.

And finally we pray for ourselves.
>	May we learn what it means to live in peace.
May we model in our own lives your way of forgiveness and reconciliation.

From the way we are with our loved ones,
>	to the way are at work, to the way we vote;
>	may we always live in peace.
Not for our sake, or for the sake of others, but for your sake,
>	as we remember the cross,
>	and live its truth into being in our world.

In the name of Jesus, we will remember
We will remember

For the feast of Christ the King

Your kingdom come, on earth as it is in heaven
Through our lives and by our prayers,
your kingdom come.

Great Christ of all love,
      in whose cross all power and authority finds its ultimate end,
we come to pray now for those earthly powers
      which determine and dictate the lives of people.

We lay before you
      those powers which present as our governing authorities.

We pray for those who work in our government and the civil service,
      and for all others at a national and local level
      who hold their delegated power on behalf of us all.
We pray also for those governments around our world
      which have put aside any notion of appropriate representation,
      and whose actions are perpetrated from base motives.

May they see through you and in us a way of being human
      that respects the other, holds authority lightly but responsibly,
      and is ever alert to the temptation to selfish misuse of power.

Grant them eyes to see, ears to hear,
      and the courage to act with compassion and mercy.

Your kingdom come, on earth as it is in heaven
Through our lives and by our prayers,
your kingdom come.

Great Christ of all love,
      in whose cross all power and authority finds its ultimate end,
We lay before you
      those powers which present as military might.

We pray for those in our armed services,
      for soldiers and generals,
      for peacekeepers and tactical forces
      for law-enforcers and legislators of law,
      and for all others whose power relies on the application of force.

FAITH IN DOUBT

We pray also for those armies and militia forces around our world,
> which have put aside any notion of appropriate force,
> and whose actions are perpetrated from base motives.

May they see through you and in us a way of being human
> that respects the other, holds authority lightly but responsibly,
> and is ever alert to the temptation to selfish misuse of power.

Grant them eyes to see, ears to hear,
> and the courage to act with compassion and mercy.

Your kingdom come, on earth as it is in heaven
**Through our lives and by our prayers,
your kingdom come.**

Great Christ of all love,
> in whose cross all power and authority finds its ultimate end,

We lay before you
> those powers which present as economic might.

We pray for those in our banks and businesses,
> for those who have personal wealth,
> and for those who handle great wealth on behalf of others.

We pray also for those economic forces around our world
> which have put aside any notion of appropriate distribution,
> and whose actions are perpetrated from base motives.

May they see through you and in us a way of being human
> that respects the other, holds authority lightly but responsibly,
> and is ever alert to the temptation to selfish misuse of power.

Grant them eyes to see, ears to hear,
> and the courage to act with compassion and mercy.

Your kingdom come, on earth as it is in heaven
**Through our lives and by our prayers,
your kingdom come.**

Amen.

For dawn after the sunset of the longest night

Loving God of the dawn and the sunset,
        we come before you this day,
        when night is longest and day is shortest,
to offer our prayers
        for those whose experience of life
        is more of darkness than it is of light.

We stand with those who live under a long shadow,
        and we join ourselves to those who struggle to see daylight.

And as we pray for others,
        we recognise that we too carry in our souls the burden of darkness.

We know that it can be true for us, as it is for others,
        that the days of brightness imperceptibly shorten
        while the nights of obscurity inexorably lengthen.

And so we pray for those who are bereaved,
        for those who have lost loved ones this year.
We feel within us the shapes of those who have gone from us,
        and we mourn their passing from our lives.

In quiet hope offered in the face of despair,
        we offer to your loving embrace
        all those whom we can no longer touch.
And we ask that you will give comfort
        where long nights of mourning seem never to come to an end.

Loving God of the dawn and the sunset,
        may darkness not overwhelm us.

We pray for those who are lonely
        for those who long for touch, for conversation,
        for friendship, for intimacy.
And we recognise in ourselves the desperate drive for companionship
        that haunts our relationships and stifles our friendships.

We ask that you will draw near to those who draw away,
        and that you will hold all who are alone in your loving embrace.

Loving God of the dawn and the sunset,
>   **may darkness not overwhelm us.**

We pray for those who are far from home
>   for those who have lost country and security
>   through war, famine, or the effects of climate change.

We pray for refugees, asylum seekers, economic migrants,
>   and all who greet the new day
>   in a country that they do not recognise as home.

May they know that you are the God of the exiles and enslaved
>   and that your welcome knows no boundaries.

Loving God of the dawn and the sunset,
>   **may darkness not overwhelm us.**

We pray for those who are lost in memories,
>   for those who are trapped in the past
>   and unable to engage the present.
We pray also for those whose memories have faded,
>   and whose experience of dementia
>   has diminished their capacity to live the day.

For all those who dream of the past,
>   we ask for healing of past hurts.
And we offer all that we are
>   to your eternal remembering.

Loving God of the dawn and the sunset,
>   **may darkness not overwhelm us.**

We pray for all that is broken in life,
>   for people, for relationships, for bodies, for objects.

And in the face of brokenness
>   we pray for healing and wholeness.

May that which is broken find its completeness in you,
>   as you bring all things to good
>   and redeem all that is damaged.

FAITH IN DOUBT

Loving God of the dawn and the sunset,
> **may darkness not overwhelm us.**

And finally we pray into the darkness,
> and we offer the hope of our voices and our hearts
> that however long the night may be, there is a new day dawning.

And we know that as the days have shortened to get us to this place,
> so they will lengthen again to take us somewhere new.

Loving God of the dawn and the sunset,
> **may darkness not overwhelm us.**

Amen.

FAITH IN DOUBT

For light and warmth on the Longest Night

Inspired by 'In the Bleak Midwinter' by Christina Rossetti

God of light and warmth, we await your coming.

We gather today at the turning of the year.
  The shortest day has been, the longest night is passing.
Tomorrow will be lighter than today.
  And imperceptibly, subtly, gradually,
  the world is moving towards summer.
God of light and warmth, we await your coming.

We gather today in a world of winter.
  We know that here will be dark days ahead,
  that there will be difficulties before us,
  that there will be snow, and rain,
  and hail, and frost, and worse.
But imperceptibly, subtly, gradually,
  the world is moving towards summer.
God of light and warmth, we await your coming.

We gather today in a world
  where your kingdom is dawning.
In the darkness of our world,
  the light of your morning is breaking.
As you came to the world that first advent,
  taking human flesh and embracing human frailty,
so you are born in us today also,
  lightening our darkness, and melting our frozen hearts.
God of light and warmth, we await your coming.

We gather today in a world
  where it can seem as if it is always winter but never Christmas.
And yet, we gather to celebrate the coming of the one
  in whom and through whom everything changes.

God of light and warmth, we await your coming,
  come Lord Jesus.

Amen.

FAITH IN DOUBT

For a world of darkness in Advent

God of Advent, in a world of chaos,
        you can be very hard to find.

The good news of your presence can seem at best a mystery.
        So teach us to wait for your unveiling,
        and give us faith to trust in your revelation.

When our world is in winter,
        comfort us with faith that the long dark nights,
        and cold hard days, do not last for eternity.

Help us to learn the lesson of the skeletal tree against the winter sky,
        and the dormant bulb in the frosted ground.

Help us to trust that new life is already nascent within our world of winter,
        and that days of darkness contain within themselves
        the assurance of your coming to all who seek you.

So today we bring before you the needs of our winter world,
        and we offer our faith in the in-breaking
        of your new season of righteousness and justice.

We pray for our planet,
        and we rejoice that some progress has been made
                on tackling climate change,
        but we recognise that there is so much still to do;
and that countries will need the courage to act against self-interest
        if genuine change is to be achieved.

Give us the courage to speak out,
        and to call your world to the self-less path which brings life.

We pray for all those who are victims of natural disasters.
        May we learn to live in ways
        that are in harmony with the natural world.

In a world of darkness, we offer our faith
        in the in-breaking of your new season of righteousness and justice.

FAITH IN DOUBT

In a world of war and terror, we pray for peace on earth.
> When nations and ideologies take up arms to fight for right,
> we find wrong on all sides.

War has created the current refugee crisis in Europe
> faced by those who have nowhere else to live,
> and people now seeking new life far from home.

But people-movement leads to fear and suspicion,
> and violence and bullying stalk the streets
> and whisper in the corridors of power.

Lord, forgive us. Help us to find a new way,
> where the spirals of violence find their end in you,

as you call us to a new way of being human
> where forgiveness trumps retaliation, and violence stops with us.

In a world of violence, we offer our faith
> in the in-breaking of your new season of righteousness and justice.

We pray for all those who suffer
> because of their faithful witness to your kingdom of peace,

and we think especially of those Christians
> who face harassment, discrimination, slander,
>> false accusation, detention, and imprisonment,
>
> because they will not turn from your path.

We pray that they will remain strong in faith and trust,
> despite physical and psychological abuse,

and that they will know your presence with them
> as they walk the costly path of the cross.

We thank you for organisations like *Release International*,
> *Action by Christians Against Torture*, and *Amnesty International*,
> as they face the darkness with unflinching gaze.

In a world of suffering, we offer our faith
> in the in-breaking of your new season of righteousness and justice.

We pray for those who find this time of year especially difficult.

We think of those who find the loss of loved ones hard to bear,
> when so many are focussing on family.

FAITH IN DOUBT

We pray for those for whom the coming Christmas festivities
    speak of unfulfilled dreams.

We ask that you will reveal yourself to those who mourn,
    and to those who are sad.

Be their comfort and joy,
    and may those of us who are happy
    be attentive to those who are not.

In a world of grief, we offer our
    faith in the in-breaking of your new season
    of righteousness and justice.

Loving God of Advent, we await your coming,
    and we anticipate your revelation,
    and we long for your unveiling.

Come, Lord Jesus, come.

Amen.

For the hope of Zechariah in Advent

Great God of unexpected endings,
> there are times when we find ourselves
>> left **speechless in wonder at the mystery of your presence**.

We pray today for and with
> all who wish to offer prayers of grateful thanksgiving
> but do not know how or to whom they should pray.

We lift up our hearts with expectant mothers and proud new fathers,
> and we rejoice with those who see in the miracle of new life
> the hope of the future of the world.

We proclaim in your name the innate equality of each child born,
> whatever their gender, nationality, ethnicity,
> social standing, or sexuality.

And we commit ourselves to seeing the image of God reflected in all,
> as we offer prayers of wonder at the miracle of life.

Great God of unexpected endings,
> there are times when we find ourselves
>> left **speechless in anticipation at the hope of your coming**.

We pray today for and with all those
> who are desperately longing for a different future,
> but who do not know how or to whom they should pray.

We offer our voices in solidarity
> with the refugees and would-be asylum seekers
> who are stranded at the border posts of Europe,

a new future before them but trapped in the silence of waiting
> for the new world to come to them and their families.

We pray especially for those who are working to alleviate suffering
> and hasten a humane solution to the crisis.

We proclaim in your name the innate equality of each human being
> who has been created in your image,

and we commit ourselves to the radical gospel vision
> of peace and reconciliation between peoples.

FAITH IN DOUBT

Great God of unexpected endings,
    there are times when we find ourselves left
speechless in powerlessness at the futility of our lives and actions.

We acknowledge before you that even after all our efforts
    the world is still not as the world should be,
and in the quiet darkness of our hearts we confess the fear
    that all our strivings have simply made things worse.
We are powerless to prevent war,
    we are powerless to stop our friends
        and loved ones from becoming ill and dying,
    we are powerless in the face of systems
        and institutions of great power
    that control far more than they have any right to.

And in the midst of the silencing of powerlessness,
    we still our hearts from panic
and we pray to hear the cry of a baby
    cutting through the babble of the world
as Christ comes to us, your words made flesh,
    salvation spoken in time and space.

Great God of unexpected endings,
    come once again to this wondering, anticipating,
    and powerless world.
Come to us in our silence.
    Come, Lord Jesus.
Come, O come, Immanuel.

Amen.

For the last night of the year

God of light and love,
    who leads us from darkness from light,
    from anger to love.

Help us to face the darkness
    in unity with those who live in that darkness,
and into the darkness of our world
    to proclaim the one who came as a child,
        fled as a refugee, and lived as an innocent one.

Help us to proclaim the one
    who came to bring light to the darkness of our world,
    to bless those who mourn, to suffer with those who suffer,
    to die with those who die,
and to bring a light that leaves nowhere to hide
    for those whose works are works of darkness.

May we who claim to be children of the light
    be those who live love.
May we who claim to be children of the light
    never turn our own faces from the darkness.
May we who claim to be children of the light
    be those who take action ourselves
    to bring light to darkness
        in the name of Christ
        and in the hope of resurrection,
    blessing those who mourn,
    bringing healing to those who suffer,
    and life to those who live in death.

Amen.

For the turning of the year

Eternal God of each present moment,
        we come before you at the turning of another year
        with diverse emotions and tentative hope.

The past and the future meet in this day,
        and lay themselves before us for prayerful pondering.

As we look back over the last year,
        we see in our lives, and in the lives of those we love,
that most human combination of joy and sorrow,
        love and loss, laughter and tears.

And so we hold before you now those whom you bring to our minds:
        loved ones we have lost, and loved ones we have discovered;
        friends who have suffered, and friends who have rejoiced;
        those who have borne burdens, and those who have found release.

And we trust that you have been present
        to all these our varied experiences of life,
        drawing all things together in your great love.

As we look to the coming year,
        we offer you our hopes and our dreams,
        our resolution and our resolve;
and yet we recognize that despite our best efforts,
        we will not be the people you have called us to be.

But we hold to the hope that by your grace
        we *will* be the people you have created us to be.

And so we pray for the uncertainty of tomorrow,
        and we trust that you will be present
            with us whatever the future may hold,
        as you draw all things together in your great love.

But most of all, we turn our prayers to the needs of this day,
        because yesterday is gone and cannot be changed,
        and tomorrow will bring enough worries of its own.

FAITH IN DOUBT

So we pray for the world to which you have come in Christ Jesus,
    bringing forgiveness where there is guilt,
    and new life where there is suffering and death.

We commit to your loving care
    all those who face tomorrow with no hope,
    because their situation today is hopeless.

And we think particularly of refugees, asylum seekers,
    and all people displaced by war or climate change.

Renew in us a concern for the weak and vulnerable,
    and give us courage:
        to speak up for the voiceless,
        to speak out against violence in all its forms,
        and to speak of the necessity to care for all creation.

We pray for those who have the authority to effect change on a global scale,
    for politicians and business leaders,
    for the rich and the powerful, the articulate and the influential.

May they be given the gift of empathy,
    and the courage to use their power
    for the good of the many, and not just the few.

Renew in us a passion for change, and an unwillingness to acquiesce.
    Give us the courage to take action
        against powers that coerce and control,
    and may we learn to be wise
        in the ways we speak and act as we seek to play our part
        in the coming of your kingdom of love, justice, and peace.

We pray for our church, for your gathered people in this place;
    we thank you for one another, in all our glorious diversity,
    and we recommit ourselves to each other
        as sisters and brothers in Christ.

We pray for all those who have come through the doors
    of this building over the last years,
    people from all walks of life, from wealth and from poverty.

FAITH IN DOUBT

We pray for all those who have joined us in worship,
    visitors from around the globe,
        bringing greetings from your worldwide family.

We pray for those who have left our fellowship,
    and for those who have joined it.

May we know, today, who we are created to be,
    and may we learn what it is
        to be true to the calling you have placed on us.

Help us to love each other,
    to welcome new people with kindness,
    to serve one another with grace,
    and to forgive one another with sincerity.

May our church, over the coming year,
    be a place of safety for those who are vulnerable,
    and a place of challenge for those who are comfortable.

May we be a community of inclusion for those who are excluded,
    and a community of defiance for those who would exclude.

May we be humble in the face of our own failings,
    but bold in the face of those who fail others.

May we be your people, in this place, at this time,
    created by you and called to live lives of courageous love.

Amen.

For Epiphany: bringing our Gold, Frankincense and Myrrh

Lord of all eternity, in whose hands are all our times,
        we come today to give you our gifts,
as people have come for millennia with gifts to offer in your service.

We are the rich and we are the poor,
        we are the strong and we are the weak,
        we are the powerful and we are the disempowered;
and we bring the offering of our lives before you
        for transformation and redemption,
        for the salvation of the world.

So we bring you our gold;
        our money, our power, and our strength.
And we rejoice that you receive our offering.

Too often in our world
        money, power and strength
        create corruption, coercion, and catastrophe.

We pray today for all those
        who are seduced by the mythology of their own success.

We pray for politicians and presidents, for monarchs and dictators,
        for those who have inherited wealth
        and for those who have acquired it.

We pray for those who rule over kingdoms,
        and whose power is beholden to money and strength.

We pray that those who hold power
        will not lose sight of the responsibility they bear
        for the weak and the vulnerable.

Just as magi brought wealth and power to your cradle,
        and you accepted the gift,
so may those with such gifts to bring in our world
        discover your willingness to receive and transform their offering.

And we recognise that we, ourselves, have to live
        with the responsibilities of our own place in that world.

FAITH IN DOUBT

Those of us with jobs, savings, and houses
    need to find in you a way of living well with our wealth,
    and so we bring our gold before you.

And we do so in faith that you are God revealed in human form.

Our offering of ourselves is not merely an act of self-transformation,
    it is an act of worship
        to the one in whom all of life finds it's beginning,
            its end, and its redemption.

You are love incarnate,
    and we worship you with all that we are and all that we have.

We bring our offering of frankincense to the God of creation.
    And as we do so, we hear the challenge
    that you bring to all other claims on our allegiance.

The clamour of the false gods is strong,
    and all too easily we are seduced
    into offering them our worship.

May we learn to resist the lures of materialism,
    the deceptions of individualism,
    and the compelling drive to competitiveness and violence.

So we pray for those who are trapped
    in servitude to these gods of our society,
    that demand ever-greater tribute, but never offer release.

May the world discover the freedom
    that is found in the God of love who gives freely to all who seek.

May the world discover the path to peace
    that opens through following the way of Jesus.

And so we worship you as our saviour,
    and as the saviour of the world.

FAITH IN DOUBT

We bring our offering of myrrh to the one who dies
    that the world might be redeemed.

We proclaim our faith that it is only in and through
    your life, death, and resurrection,
    that our own lives acquire meaning.

And so we pray for all those seeking meaning to their lives;
    for searchers and seekers, for the curious and the questioners.
May they hear in your story,
    the path towards freedom, love, and eternal acceptance.

We pray for our friends and our families,
    for those we meet and those we avoid.

Help us to remember that it is not our calling to save others,
    but rather that it is our vocation
to live out our own salvation before the world,
    always pointing to the one in whom
    the God of love is made fully known.

In weakness and in strength,
    in poverty and in power,
        in loneliness and in love,
    we offer our prayers to the one in whom all our times are held.

Amen.

For the wisdom of the Magi at Epiphany

Loving God of unexpected revelation,
>we remember today the visit of the magi to the infant Christ;

and in this story we see the breaking down of barriers
>that divided Jew from Gentile,
>rich from poor, vulnerable from powerful.

And yet we look at our world, and we see nation turned against nation,
>we see the gap between wealth and poverty widening,
>and we see the powerful exploiting the vulnerable.

So teach us, today, the wisdom of the magi,
>that we might be strengthened to the task
>of living your alternative world of justice and reconciliation
>into being in the midst of our world.

God of the magi,
>give us wisdom to follow your leading,

even when the call of the good news takes us in the opposite direction
>to the way the world seems to be going.

We pray specifically for those in our world
>who are seduced by ideologies of nationalism and segregation;

who seek to enforce borders and boundaries
>in ways that divide humanity into ever smaller clusters
>of self-interest and protection.

We pray for all those who now feel unwelcome or threatened
>in the place they have come to call home;

for migrants and immigrants, for asylum seekers and refugees,
>for the children and grandchildren
>of those who came to our country in previous generations.

We confess our society's sins of exclusion and segregation,
>and we pray that our politicians and leaders
>>will have generous hearts,
>>inclusive policies, and a love for difference
>>>that reflects the diversity of humanity.

We recognise that the change begins with us,
> and so we ask for your grace that we too might find ways
> of including and welcoming those whom others would exclude.

God of the magi,
> give us generosity to offer our gifts to your service.

From the treasure-store of our hearts and minds
> we offer our humility and our service, our time and our talents.

We recognise that we live in a world
> where we are so often encouraged
>> to focus first on ourselves and our own,
> and yet we know that society is enriched
>> when people give with no expectation of reward.

So free us from the temptation to selfish behaviour,
> and give us a generosity of spirit,
>> that drives us towards the other rather than away from them.

We pray, with gratitude, for the charities that serve our city,
> and for those who volunteer in them.
We give thanks for those who give time to care, to love, and to serve.

So we pray for the work of …, and all our other partners
> who give so much to bring about good news in our area.

God of the magi,
> we offer our gifts of wealth.

Such as we have them,
> we offer our personal money and our individual power;
and as a community, we offer our church's resources to your service,
> from our buildings and investments,
>> to our reputation and our influence.

We recognise that we have responsibilities to fulfil
> in the way we hold and handle our wealth,
and yet we also know that you call us to a life of adventure and risk-taking
> as we seek to embody your gospel of good news for all people.

FAITH IN DOUBT

So give us wisdom to be careful, and courage to be generous,
        and may the offering of our gold be a blessing to many.

We pray for those in our world who handle great wealth,
        and we think particularly of those
        who work in banking and business.
May they discover your wisdom
        to bring justice and reconciliation
        into being through the resources they control.

God of the magi,
        we offer our gifts of worship.
We lay aside all other claims on our devotion,
        and we focus our attention on your revelation in Jesus Christ.

We recognise the temptation to idolatry is always before us,
        and we know that we have a seemingly endless capacity
            to project our own desires onto you,
            and worship them instead of you.

So keep our eyes fixed on Jesus,
        who always calls us beyond ourselves.

May we be daily challenged
        to behave in ways that are inspired by the life of Jesus,
loving others as we love ourselves,
        forgiving those who cause us hurt,
and offering our hearts, and souls, and minds, and strength to your service.

We pray for those who do not have freedom of worship around our world,
        and we hold before you today the persecuted church.
Be especially close to those who are imprisoned for their faith;
        and may we never take our own freedom
        to worship you for granted.

God of the magi,
>	we offer our gifts of empathy, our emotions and our love.
In a world which so often turns away from the needs
>	of those who are hurting and damaged,
>>	help us to face the darkness with those who live in darkness.

We are thankful for those who have stood alongside us
>	when we have needed loving support,
>>	and we commit ourselves to offering that same love to others.

We thank you for the example of Jesus,
>	who brought wholeness to those who were broken,
and who restored to community
>	those who were cut off from others.
May we, in this church, be a people of restorative love.

We pray for those who are bereaved, for those who are unwell,
>	and for those who are struggling with life.
We pray particularly today for …

All these prayers we offer, in the name of Jesus our saviour.

Amen.

For patience in the darkness of night

Romans 8.25
"If we hope for what we do not see,
we wait for it with patience"

Creative God of each day's new dawn,
    infuse the darkness of our lives
    with the light of your presence.

May your strength grow brighter, hour by hour,
    until the darkness of the night is a lost dream.

So help us to work out our salvation,
    minute by minute, hour by hour, day by day.

And as day gives way to night,
    and light fades to darkness,
may the hope of your dawning
    sustain us through the night terrors.

Because we hope for what we do not yet see,
    and we wait with patience,
    because we have no other choice.

Amen.

For Intercessions at a Baptism

Loving God of living water,
> we come now to pray for ourselves and for your world.

In Christ, you meet us in the everyday stuff of our lives.

As you once entered the waters of the Jordan at your own baptism,
> so you continue to immerse yourself
> in the daily reality of our humanity.

As you once met us in the waters of our own baptism,
> so you are joined with us each moment
> in our need for forgiveness, renewal, and transformation.

And so we take this opportunity, this day,
> to reaffirm before you the promises made at our own baptisms.

We pray especially for … and …
> who have been baptised here today.

Together, as your people,
> we recommit ourselves to the path of faithful discipleship,

we seek forgiveness for those times
> where we have been less than we should have been,

and we offer ourselves once again to the task of becoming your people,
> for the salvation of the world.

Loving God of living water,
> we pray for all those who need your cleansing touch.

We pray for those whose path in this life
> has taken them far from the life-giving way of Christ.

We pray for those whose courage has failed,
> and whose will has been lacking.

We pray for those who have heard your voice
> inviting them to join you in the life-giving water,
> but who have turned away and followed their own path.

We pray for our friends, and for our families.
> We pray for those known to us only by their reputation.

Lord, draw near to those who draw away from you.

Loving God of living water,
> we pray for a world where death so often gets the last word.

We lift before you now those places and people known to us
> where death seems to have the upper hand,
> and where life seems stifled and suppressed.

FAITH IN DOUBT

We pray for those living with illness,
    and especially for those who know
        that their time remaining on this earth
    is less than they would have hoped for.
Living Lord, draw near to them as they draw nearer to you in death.

Through the promises of baptism and resurrection,
    may they know that life is more than death,
    and that your love endures through and beyond the tomb.

We pray also for those situations around the world
    where death and disaster overtake a population.
We pray especially today for Syria, for Iraq and Iran, for Palestine,
    and for other places and peoples known to us
    where death seems victorious. …

Living Lord of resurrection promise,
    may streams of life-giving water come to the deserts of destruction.
May justice flow like rivers, and righteousness like a never failing stream.

We also commit to your loving care all those
    whose faithful commitment to their baptismal promises
    has led them to persecution and death.
We lift before you now those situations around the world
    where Christians are targeted for no other reason
    than their unyielding identification with the God of love
        made known in Christ Jesus.
May new life come to many through their faithful witness.

Loving God of living water,
    we thank you that you step down
        into the midst of the mess of this world,
    and into the complexities of our own lives.
We thank you that in baptism,
    you draw near to us and invite us to draw near to you.
We thank you that you do not leave the world unchanged,
    and that you are daily at work,
        inviting transformation, and bringing hope and new life.

Amen.

For Pride Sunday

God of love, justice, and welcome,
    we bring before you today the deep longing of our hearts
        for the world in which we live,
    and our concerns for those whose experience of this world
        is marred by the actions of others.

This weekend of Pride, we hold in our prayers all those
    who are discriminated against
    because of their sexuality or gender.

We believe that you love and care for all people,
    and that whatever our orientation
    you are ready to embrace us in love.

We thank you that we live in a country where freedoms to express
    our God-given sexuality and identity are protected,
and we lament that there are still many countries
    where same sex relationships are criminalised.

We confess the role that the Christian church has played
    in shaping homophobic and discriminatory
    laws and cultures over the centuries,
and we commit ourselves as a congregation of your people
    to the ongoing task of challenging our own attitudes
        to difference and discrimination,
    and to speaking out the truth as it is revealed to us.

So we pray for those LGBTQ Christians
    who find themselves excluded from faith communities;
for those who experience damage
    to their mental health and spiritual wellbeing
    from the abusive expectations of other Christians.

FAITH IN DOUBT

We hold in prayer those coerced into denying their sexuality,
    those who have found themselves in loveless marriages,
    and those who have remained single and celibate
        against their calling or desires.

We give thanks for those who reveal through their lives
    the great diversity of humanity made in your image,
and we confess the sin of normalising
    one subjective experience of 'ourselves'
    in ways that diminish others' experience of 'their selves'.

So we pray for those who have had the courage to take a stand
    for LGBTQ inclusion in both society and church life.

We recognise that without challenge, nothing changes,
    and so we stand in prayer alongside those
    who have found the strength to bring such challenge
        even at great personal cost.

We hold before you those who continue to speak out,
    challenging complacency and highlighting homophobic violence,
and we lament the many other less visible discriminations
    that mark the day to day existence of the LGBTQ community.

We pray for those who speak courageously in church communities,
    seeking to ensure that your family is place where all are welcome.

We commend to your care those who offer faithful witness
    within churches where same sex attraction is condemned as sinful,
    and who regularly hear condemnations of their identity.

We hold before you those who are called to serve in Christian ministry,
    but who are denied recognition and ordination.

We think of churches divided against each other and within themselves,
    and we know that the body of Christ is broken,
    and the blood of Christ is spilled.

We give thanks for organisations such as *Christians at Pride*, *Affirm*,
> *One Body One Faith*, the *Two:23 Network*,
and other organisations which offer a faithful LGBTQ voice
> within the structures and systems of Christian life and witness.

We thank you for clergy who have spoken up
> in support of same sex marriage and LGBTQ inclusion.

And we give thanks for those in our own church family
> who offer a persistent challenge for us to never be complacent.

We pray for those who have entered
> into same sex marriages in this building,
and we give thanks for those other churches
> which have taken a public stand on inclusion.

We bring all these our prayers before you,
> and we commit ourselves to the task of bringing into being
> your kingdom of love, justice and welcome,
> on earth, as it is in heaven.

Amen.

For those getting married

Great God of eternal love, we rejoice with you
        that today ... and ... have joined themselves to one another
        in love, commitment, and marriage.

May the love they share always reflect your own loving nature.

May they know the peace that comes from acceptance,
        the joy that comes from forgiveness,
        and the hope that comes from faithfulness.

Grant them the gifts of grace
        that sustain through the times of difficulty,
        and which open the path to a yet more loving future.

We thank you that their marriage is also a blessing to others,
        a symbol and sign of something greater than itself.

We pray for their friends and families,
        and the communities in which they will live.

Together we offer our hopes, our dreams, and our love;
        confident that your self-giving, ceaseless Spirit
        will work in and through ... and ...
        to make your love known.

Amen.

For remembering that nothing is lost

Great God of all love,
    we come before you this afternoon
        to give thanks for the life of …, who has died.

We come to remember, to tell again some of the stories of their life;
    and as we share with one another,
we know that we also share with you
    not only our sadness at their passing,
    but also the precious joy and laughter of their life.

We rejoice that, in you, nothing that is good is ever lost,
    and that within your great love,
        all our lives continue to be joined to that of …,
        as we are joined to one another.

And so we gather to proclaim the resurrection of Christ Jesus,
    in whom we encounter life eternal,
    and in whom all human mortality is transfigured.

So, great God of all love, grant us today the peace of your risen son,
    that our fears may be dispelled,
    our tears eased, and our lives renewed.

All this we pray because of Christ Jesus our Lord.

Amen.

For the world at a time of mourning

God of love, giver and holder of life eternal,
> as we have gathered to remember the life of … who has died,
> so we come now to pray for your world.

We bring our prayers for new life,
> joining our yearnings with the force of your love,
> that that world may be transformed.

We pray first for all those who mourn,
> and we ask that you will draw near to them in their loss.

May it be true for them that the comfort of your love
> reaches to the depths of their bereavement,
> to bring healing and wholeness.

We pray especially for the family and friends of …
> We own before you our emotions, and our grief at their passing.

We are grateful to you for all that they have been to us,
> for the distinctive contribution that they have brought
> > to our lives and our communities,
> and for their faithfulness to you in the face of illness.

We miss them, and we are sad that they are gone from us.
> We commit them to your eternal care,
and trust that their life will be held within your eternal embrace of love.

We pray also for all those
> who live in situations of hopelessness and despair.

We pray for exiles in our world;
> for those who have been displaced
> from the lives, families, and workplaces that they cherish and value.

We think particularly of those
> who have been forced to flee because of the civil war,
and we pray for those who are working
> for long term peace and stability.

FAITH IN DOUBT

May it be true for them
> that you are the God who brings
> the hope and possibility of restoration.

Breathe your spirit of new life
> into the lives of those whose faith in the future has faded.

We pray for the enslaved of our world;
> and we think particularly of those
>> who have been trafficked to our country,
> and are currently living within our city as effective slaves
>> to industries that demean and objectify their humanity.

May they find in you a God who values them,
> and may they find through your people an acceptance and love
>> that mirrors your eternal love,
> and a commitment to liberation and new life
>> that mirrors the freedom of your Spirit.

We pray also for those who are enslaved to addictions,
> and are unable to break the hold
>> of destructive patterns of behaviour on their lives.

We ask that they will find liberation in you,
> and we pray particularly for the various anonymous groups
> who open a path to freedom and new life.

God of love, giver and holder of life eternal,
> we bring these our prayers for new life,
joining our yearnings with the force of your love,
> that that world may be transformed.

Amen.

For the celebration of a Golden Wedding

Great God of love,
We rejoice that fifty years ago,
    you called … and …
    into a covenant of marriage.

We pause now in the midst of our celebrations
    to offer you our gratitude.

We are thankful for their love for each other,
    and for you;
We are thankful for their family, and their friends,
    for faithfulness and fortitude.

And as we share food and drink together now,
    we offer this time, and this day, to you.

We remember those who go without,
    and those whose lives are in difficulty this day.
We remember those who cannot be here today
    and we think particularly of the people of …

Bless us with your love,
    may we be agents of your peace and hope.
Bless this food to our bodies,
    and sanctify our time together.

For the sake of Jesus Christ
    our Lord and Saviour.

Amen.

WORDS OF BLESSING

How we end a worship service is surely as important as how we begin it.

My normal practice is to use the following blessing, which is one I learned and internalised many decades ago:

'Go into God's world,
      with love, hope, faith, and joy in your hearts;
And may the blessing of Almighty God,
      Creator, Redeemer, and Sustainer,
Be with you today, and for ever more.
Amen.'

However there are occasions where different words are called for, and these blessings have taken shape as I have sought to find ways of sending the congregation out into the world to embody in their lives the encounter we have had with God in worship.

For love, faith, and hope

May the Creator of love give us new hope.
May the son of hope give us new faith.
May the spirit of faith give us new love.
So go in love, faith and hope,
and may the blessing of God rest with us all.
Amen.

For service, love, and forgiveness

May Jesus Christ your friend and redeemer
> give you the Power to serve
May the Holy Spirit your sustainer
>give you the Power to love
May God your creator
>give you the Power to forgive and to know forgiveness.
May the Almighty God: creator, redeemer, and sustainer,
>be with us all, evermore.
Amen

For the community of God

May God the three-in-one,
>who binds us together in community as one body,
fire us by the Spirit,
>inspire us to live the life of the Son,
and indwell us with the love of our divine parent;
>this day and for evermore.
Amen

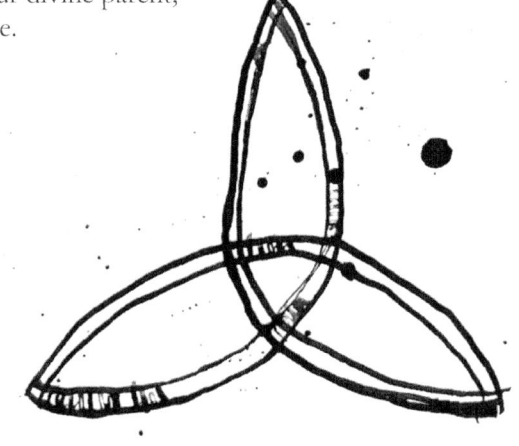

The breath of Christ

May the peace of Christ
        be with you.
May the mind of Christ
        give shape to your thoughts.
May the emptiness of Christ
        release you.
May the equality of Christ
        diminish you.
May the likeness of Christ
        ennoble you.
May the death of Christ
        be your death.
May the exaltation of Christ
        revive you.
May the name of Christ
        cause you to draw breath.

For grace, faith, and peace

Almighty God of hidden hope,
        grant us grace.
Loving Christ of the coming kingdom,
        grant us faith.
Living Spirit of new life,
        grant us peace.
And may the blessing of the presence of God,
        creator, redeemer, and sustainer,
        be with us all, today and evermore.
Amen.

For the end of the day

God of the day and the night,
    God of the morning and the evening,
God of new life, and God of our lives,
    We commit ourselves to your loving embrace,
Grant us peace.
Amen.

For a troubled world

Come, loving Christ,
    to our world of illness and isolation.
Bring wholeness to the broken,
    comfort to the grieving, and peace to the troubled.
May we, your people,
    be inspired to acts of faith and service in your name.
Amen.

For Good Friday

May the blessing of God the Almighty,
    God the Crucified, and God the Eternal,
be with us and sustain us
    on this day of darkness and death.
Amen.

For a Wedding

Great God of eternal love,
We ask your blessing on all who seek to live in love.
Bless friendships, partnerships, and marriages;
    Bless peacemakers and harmonisers;
Bless colleagues and collaborators;
    Bless … and bless …
And may the God of eternal love,
    be with each one of us,
    today, and for ever more.
Amen.

WORDS OF DOUBT AND FAITH

Eugene Peterson has suggested that every preacher should be a poet, and mostly I find that this takes the form of the words I use in sermons and prayers. But occasionally I also try to write actual poems, perhaps to capture a moment of humour, experience, reflection, or crisis.

Scripture reminds us that doubt and faith go hand in hand: we see 'through a glass darkly', we search 'believing' while crying out to the Lord to help our unbelief. So I hope these poems and stories will evoke in us all a prayerful and faith-full response.

Sheep and Goats

'Stop the world,' said the king, 'I'm getting confused.
        Let's take five, simmer down, and think…

'I'm trying to decide, and it just isn't clear,
        on the difference between goats and sheep.'

'I know,' cried a voice,
        'I think it's to do with the people you meet
        and the things that you do.

'If you're kind to the poor, and give food from your table,
        and care where you're able,
'I'm pretty sure you are a sheep.'

'Hark at him bleating on,' came a second response,
        'he's full of his own self-importance.

'I'm afraid it's more complex than that.
        It's not what you do to the poor that decides,
        it's the attitude with which you do it.

'A sheep must be holy and humble
        and so, if you're anything else you're a goat.'

'That's just woolly thinking,' the first voice replied,
        'if anyone's goat-ish it's you.

'It's all very well being holy and such,
        but that doesn't get anyone fed.'

Said the goat to the sheep,
        'I think we've resolved it,
        the sheep looks like me and the goat looks like you.'

'I see it the same,' came the answer right back,
        'a ewe looks like me not like you.'

'Hang on,' said the king, 'I'm still no more clear.
        Are you both sure and certain you're sheep?'

FAITH IN DOUBT

'Why yes,' cried two voices, both speaking as one,
    'we know that we're sheep, and we're sure it must be,
    for we know that they all must be goats.'

'So let me be clear,' said the king with a sigh,
    'you each want the other condemned?

'Well it's never so clear. And I'm never so sure.
    And there's something that still gets my goat:

'You've heard of the herd, the tribe, and the nation;
    the people who act just like you?

'Well, the herd is a fable we're able to tell,
    just to justify me and my own.

'If you think you're all sheep, and that others are goats,
    you divide up the world very wrong.'

Then the king turned away, and went on his way,
    and restarted the world once again.

But after a minute he paused in his stride,
    and looked over his shoulder,
    to see who was following on.

Waiting for the lightness

'Wait', you said,
'Ok', said I.
And the silence hung heavy
For a while.

'That's quite a burden', you said.
'Quite', said I,
'I picked it up somewhere,
Along the way.'

'Wait', you said.
'Yes', said I,
'This weight is heavy,
And it's dragging me down'

'Lighten up', you said,
'Ok', said I,
But the light was hard to find
And the darkness weighed in.

'Let it be lighter', you said,
And it was,
And it was good.

Assisi see

Saint Francis of Assisi-si
Went to see what he could see, see, see.
But all Assisi saw, saw, saw,
Was Jesus in the faces of the poor, poor, poor.

Doubt

'Whither goest thou?' Jesus asked.

'Whence comest thou?' Job replied.

'Don't you know?' Jesus asked.

'Don't you?' Job replied.

'I wasn't really talking to you.' Jesus said.

'Nor I you.' Job replied.

'But anyway, since we're here, where are you off to?' Jesus asked.

'Not telling.' Said Job.

'If you don't know, that's fine.' Said Jesus.

'Same to you.' Said Job.

'The wind of the Spirit blows whither it will.' Said Jesus.

'You canst not tell whence it cometh.' Replied Job

'Nor whither it goeth.' Added Jesus.

'But thou canst hearest the sound thereof.' Said Job.

'Yes.' Replied Jesus.

I saw a man

Where?
There, on the stair!

Where on the stair?
Right there!

A little man, with holes in his shoes,
asleep on the steps of my church.

A man barely visible as I rush by,
the rain going drip drippety drop
on our hair and our faces.

But it was a man, I'm sure.
A man like me.

But so not like me,
it was hard to tell.

And then he was gone.
Or I was.

Autumn

I know you're not supposed to have favourites,
But mine has always been Autumn.

Neither too hot nor cold;
With just enough bitter melancholy
To offset the blithe optimism of Spring.

Everything dying,
gloriously, slowly;
Leaves surrendering to rust.

Trees lifting their bare arms
In bleak surrender.

Life lies dormant,
Disguised as death.

Darkness dominant
And days diminished.

There is great beauty is a good ending,
As any author will tell you.

But still the leaves remain:
Dry on the ground
for kicking and shuffling,
Soaked and sodden for rotting to nothing.

The leaves remain,
and are reborn.
Leaves for healing,
Leaves for hope.

So if I am allowed a favourite,
I choose Autumn.

The Umpire

'You lose", said the umpire one sunny afternoon.
'You tried, and you lost. You loser.'

'But what were the rules?' I asked, in fear.
And the Umpire spelled them out:
'You can try, but you'll fail;
You can fight, but you'll falter;
And nothing will ever be enough.'

'So who wrote the rules?' I dared to enquire.
'Well you did, of course', they replied,
'You cut them deep in your soul, one dark afternoon.'

'But what can I do to be free?' I said.
And the umpire stared at me hard.

And the longer I looked,
And the harder they stared,
The more I saw me looking back.

I Doubt

I doubt,
therefore I believe;

Of this I am certain:
nothing.

Am I right?
Of course I am;

or at least I think I am.

I think,
therefore I think I am right.

After all,
who on earth thinks they are wrong?

But. I am also logical.
And I know this:
I have been wrong before.

So: I may be wrong again.

Today's thoughts
are not yesterday's thoughts.

So tomorrow
will bring different thoughts.

Today's truth
is true today.

But truth is relative;
and only doubt is faithful.

Maybe only the faithless
doubt doubt.

So I, for my part,
will believe in doubt.

We

A lifetime sentence,
never spoken
to completion.

A poem
unfinished;
free in form,
but stable
in structure.

We are
joined,
you
and
I,
by
an
invisible
thread;
together
whatever,
wherever
we tread.

'I do'
did it up,
and what has been joined
shall not be undone.

We were bound to be together;
the knot was tied tight.
We are held fast.

If we are parted for a time,
thread stretched
by wandering feet,
which may become yards,
miles, continents even;
we shall be distanced
but never distant,
parted but not apart.

Beatitudes not Platitudes

Blessed are those who refuse the lie
> that one life is worth more than any other,
for theirs is the future of humanity.

Blessed are those who have stared long into the abyss,
for theirs is honesty beyond grief.

Blessed are those who resist retaliation,
for the earth will never be won by force.

Blessed are those who would rather die for truth
> than live with compromise,
for the truth will outlive all lies.

Blessed are those who forgive the unforgivable,
for they have seen the darkness of their own souls.

Blessed are those who know themselves truly,
for they have seen themselves as God sees them.

Blessed are those who are provocatively nonviolent,
for they are following the path of the son of God.

Blessed are those who choose to receive violence but not to give it,
for the future is born out of such choices.

Blessed are you when you stand up for truth
and hell itself decides to try and destroy you.
You're not the first and you won't be the last.

I'm telling you now, nothing makes any sense
> unless you learn see it differently,
and then choose to live that alternative into being.

March 1, 2017

February fades and
spring marches in;
random rows
of snowdrops and daffodils,
all lent an air of precision by
roses, prim- and proper-
budding hope of new life.

December 21, 2016

Long night ahead,
or just a short day?

It's not the hours of darkness
that bother me,
but the passing of the light.

Life's little day
ebbing too swiftly
to its close.

The years blink past,
and light dims to dark.

But the light of new life
will soon flicker
in a baby's eyes.

The eternal baby:
every year crucified,
every year reborn.

New life
in the cycle of life:
light returns,
and death is undone.

Bible Bashing

Today,
I tore a Bible to shreds.
I bashed a Bible to bits.

Today was a day
Of anger,
And pain,
And overwhelming disappointment.

Today,
Preaching is pointless,
Unappreciated,
Unbiblical,
Worthless.

Today,
Faith lies shredded
To tatters.
A mess
of anger,
And pain,
And disappointment.

Today,
Ministry is meaningless.
People don't want to change.
People don't want change.
There is no transformation
Just power games.

And today,
the Bible
sits in bits,
in a bag
by the bin.

This flesh made words

> *A poem inspired by John 1.14*
> *"And the word became flesh"*

Too thin,
too fat,
too short,
too slim,
too dark,
too grey,
too white,
too light,
too chubby,
too bubbly,
too old,
too young,
too tired
to care,
too much
to do
today,
too stressed
to embrace
tomorrow,
too loud
to hear,
too cynical
to see,
too stupid
to know,
too arrogant
to be known,
too busy
to be,
too human
to be me.

The leaves are for the healing of the nations

The Spirit gave up with a gentle whimper,
grown hoarse from too much whispering.

The wilderness was a big place for a lone voice,
and it took effort to keep calm and small and still.

So the a Spirit stopped trying.
'Let them be deaf, and I shall be dumb', she said.

And do you know, the people didn't notice.
Not straight away.
Not today, or tomorrow.

But in time,
in time and in due course,
the world grew colder,
less connected,
less alive.

And the voice no-one had heard was missed,
and the earthquake came,
and the loud winds blew,
and the fires raged.

And the Spirit was nowhere to be found.

Until one morning,
not long before the end,
a gentle wind stirred the leaves of the tree,
and fluttered the leaves of the book,
and everyone stopped.

And everyone noticed.
And the wind in the leaves
was for the healing of the nations.

This World

This world is a trick of my mind's eye.
This body a form of endless deception.
Equality is a myth,
and exploitation abounds.

Life is emptiness personified;
and we are all slaves,
every last human one of us.

We are lost, and are not found;
obedient in our humble servitude,
to the day we die.

Exaltation is an unattainable dream,
and names are but whispers of being
like wind in reeds that bend and break.

Heaven calls us
and Earth calls us back.
Our tongues speak our hope of glory,
and the void listens.

A quest for meaning

Meaning hides
in the gaps between words,
while letters shape
the space into which they fall.

We know nothing,
which is probably where knowledge begins.

So run from certainty,
and flee definition.

Seek God where God cannot be found;
and do not, under any circumstances, do what you are told.

Provoking Faith

> *I was challenged to write this hymn by one of our church members, as a way of expressing together our church vision statement: 'Provoking faith in the heart of London'.*

Verse 1
We are your people called together,
Bringing hearts and minds to you;
We nurture faith through strength and weakness,
Seeking truth in all we do.

Chorus
Great God you call us to your heart-beat:
Living love, including all;
Provoking faith across our city,
Help us follow where you call.

Verse 2
Great Christ our centre and our focus
Give us courage to stand true;
Confronting forces of injustice,
Risking all, we follow you.

Verse 3
This church stands open to your Spirit,
We will help the broken mend;
A sanctuary for those excluded,
Christ, we follow to the end.

> *To hear a recording of this hymn, sung by the Bloomsbury Lockdown Choir to the new tune written by Alexandra Cran-McGreehin, please visit: www.bloomsbury.org.uk/a-new-hymn-for-bloomsbury*

Everlasting

Everlasting to everlasting;
eternity to eternity;
moment by moment.

Life is a mystery of being,
a constant quest for meaning.

Tired old bones struggle onwards
while the spirit leaps to new heights.

Faith grows stronger even as it dies,
and hope will not quiet down.

And in all this, love persists,
hunting each second
and bringing home it's quarry.

Rublev

We gathered around the oak:
no leaves; no life;
summer gone;
winter come.

We shared
bread from a harvest long past,
and wine from vines now barren.

Remnants of joy.
Yet there on the dead oak
the tiny buds of hope
gave promise.

And we laughed.

The step of faith

In gratitude for Terry Pratchett

"Mind how you go",
said the old woman.
And she knew the importance of this advice.

Each step is a gift,
each stride to be measured and treasured.
Each stumble and slip a peril.

So, be careful:
Be full of care,
and be mindful of how you go.

Notice the now.
Look at the path
as well as the view.

Walk well on the earth
for as long as the path lasts.

And at the end
Take heart, and do not be afraid.

Go well with God.

As the old woman said,
"Mind how you go."

The open road

From birth to death,
From here to there,
From now until eternity.

From dawn to dusk,
From past to future,
From peak to trough and back again.

Moment by moment we live:
Snapshots of instant existence,
Flickering so fast they blur our lives.

But. Stop.
Now. Is. The. Moment.

Receive the gift of the present,
And do not pass it by.

OK

It's OK
to be not OK.
So they say.
But it's not OK
to be not OK,
if you insist
on being not OK
your way.

If you're OK,
it's OK to be you,
But if you're not OK,
then it's not OK
to be true to you.

But you are OK
Being not OK.
OK?

Ice & Fire

A poem for Advent Sunday, 2015

Lukewarm life like a bath;
soporific drug of meaninglessness?

Never.

Better cold like ice,
better frozen in heart,
and mind, and soul.

Better strong and brittle.
Better something than nothing.

Better hot like fire.
Better burn out,
than flicker into nothing.

Better a blaze of glory,
better heat and fury,
better furnace and judgement.

Come ice, come fire:
strengthen and purify.

Cool self-righteous anger.
Enflame righteousness.

Come ice, come fire.

Still Now

It's still now.
Present perfected.
Past action repeated.
Captured moments.
Keeping time.
Here again.
Nothing lost.
Still now.

Greenbelt

My natural spiritual home:
Ten thousand misfits:
Refugees from 'reality'.

An oasis of grace
In the desert of the real.

A place of transcendence
A homecoming welcome
Acceptance and doubting
And longing and shouting.

Reviving rebellion,
Resourcing subversion,
At home in the fields.

The land

One well-aimed stone
was all that it took
for a young boy
to slay Goliath.

The Philistine defeated
and the land secured.

One well-aimed stone
was all that it took
for a young soldier
to tear-gas a teenager.

Is this Palestine defeated
And the land secured?

One well-aimed stone
can bring down an empire,
or start a war,
or secure freedom.

One stone
can shatter a wall.

One stone
can become the cornerstone.

One stone
can ransom a kingdom.

One stone
can lay the foundations
for a new world.

A square peg

A square peg in a round hole
A spiritual misfit
Never fully belonging
Never quite at home

Always one step ahead
or one step behind

The cynical edge
The questioning glance

Is this what it means
to be a prophet?

Is this what it means
to be a disciple of the one
who had nowhere to lay his head?

Is this what it means
to be a follower of the mendicant misfit
who said:
'A prophet has no honour at home'…?

But
Maybe
a prophet with honour is never at home…
Maybe
the call is to never settle
Maybe
the call is to journey, to run, to hide, to escape

To forever be
the square peg in the round hole.

All things bright and beautiful

Tics that carry Lyme disease
Are made by God as well;
Things that make us ill at ease,
And make our armpits swell.
Survival of the fittest
Is part of how things work;
Immunity is needed
To fight off other germs.

This evil generation

"When an email has gone out of an inbox, it wanders through waterless regions looking for a resting place, but it finds none. Then it says, 'I will return to my house from which I came.' When it comes, it finds it empty, swept, and put in order. Then it goes and brings along seven other emails more evil than itself, and they enter and live there; and the last state of that inbox is worse than the first.

That is the way it is with this evil generation."

Masks

Prophylactics
inexpertly applied.
Obscene little noses,
poking out
above lowered fabric.
Warm chins,
but no hot lips.
It's indecent exposure.

Vaccination

Before the nations he has bared his holey arm.

The Parable of the Theatre

The kingdom of heaven is like this.

A theatre was putting on a wonderful production;
>everyone would enjoy it,
>>and the standing ovation would be rapturous.

Some people heard about the production early,
>and quickly bought their seats in the stalls.

Some people could not afford the best seats,
>and instead bought cheap seats on benches up in the gods.

Some people left it until the last minute
>and bought reduced price tickets at the door.

When the performance was due to start, the stalls were not full.

So those with cheap seats were moved down to the stalls
>alongside the rich and the cultured.

The show was magnificent,
>but those who had bought their tickets early tutted
and spent the performance composing in their heads
>>letters of complaint to the management
>>about how unfair it all was.

The Parable of the Waiting Room

The kingdom of heaven is like this.

Some people arrived early for the train, not wanting to miss it,
    and quickly took their seats in the waiting room.

Gradually the waiting room filled up,
    and once all the seats had been taken,
    people stood crowded in the middle of the room.

When the train arrived, everyone got on;
    but those who arrived last were the first onto the train,
    and took all the seats.

Those who had arrived early
    ended up standing all the way to the destination.

'The Sign of the Time'

    - a poem for Advent

Divine Time is not a line,
from Earth to Heaven,
from Hell to redemption,
from here to there.

Divine Time is a circle;
a spiral of turning.

As the seasons turn the year,
the hands of Divine Time
proscribe their journey
from start to start,
and from end to end.

Now is the start,
and now is the end.

'Eternity in each present moment'.

Blind Bartimaeus

It's not very far from Jerusalem to Jericho,
but it's a long way back again.

Those few miles can take a lifetime.

Jerusalem, the city of dreams;
Jericho, the city of nightmares.

In Jerusalem, anything seems possible;
in Jericho, your dreams turn to pillars of salt,
and the water of the sea has no life in it.

The road from Jerusalem to Jericho and back is dangerous;
men get set upon by robbers.

I made it through once, but then I got stuck.

Dusty existence,
neither mercy nor reprieve, was my lot;
a path ending at the dead shores of the sea.

But I have kept faith;
unseeing eyes scanning a way through the wilderness.

And one day the way found me.

I Do Believe

God help me, I do not believe…

I do not believe in God the Father.
I do not believe in a virgin birth.
I do not believe in three wise men, choirs of angels, or singing shepherds.
I do not believe in a reanimated corpse.
I do not believe that praying changes God, or his mind.
I do not believe in eternal damnation,
      or in hell as the eternal destiny of the faithless.
I do not believe in Heaven as the eternal destination of the faithful.
I do not believe that Jesus will come again.
I do not believe people are called to do anything.
I do not believe in a God of war, violence, hatred or division.
I do not believe in a God who is angry, vicious, vengeful, or wrathful.
I do not believe eternal life is the spiritual equivalent
      of a final salary pension scheme;
      a person's state of grace at the point of death
      is not the ultimate determination of their eternal soul.
I do not believe that on the cross Jesus died to pay the price for my sins.
I do not believe that speaking in tongues
      is the indicator of the Spirit's presence.
I do not believe you have to be 'born again' to be saved.
I do not believe in original sin.
I do not believe the Bible is the word of God.
      If you want God's words in written form, read the Koran.
I do not believe that marriage must be between one man and one woman.
I do not believe in 'creation', with or without an 'ism'.
I do not believe in one holy catholic and apostolic church.

But I do still believe, God help me…

I believe that God is the mother and father of us all,
      the ground of our being,
      and the source of all that makes us human.
I believe that God is love, and that in God there is no darkness at all.
I believe in resurrection through Christ Jesus,
      and that death does not get the final word on life.
I believe that those who are in Christ are daily born again from above.
I believe in hell as a present reality; as, I suspect,
      do the countless multitudes who find themselves trapped there.

FAITH IN DOUBT

I believe that idolatry is the root cause of all sin,
    and that wherever God is displaced from the centre of the cosmos,
    the path to hell opens before us.
I believe that through Christ's body people are redeemed from hell
    and released from satan's power.
I believe that the eternal value of a person's life
    does not depend on their appreciation of their own eternal worth.
I believe that God is most fully and uniquely
    revealed in the person of Christ,
    and that those who know Christ, know God.
I believe that the Spirit of Christ is with all those who follow him,
    revealing him in and through those
    who bear faithful witness to him.
I believe that Christ died to save humanity
    from the twin powers of sin and death.
I believe that prayer changes everything, starting with me.
I believe that people are called to be, and then to live out that calling.
I believe that the kingdom of heaven
    is an in-breaking reality of transformation.
I believe that Jesus comes again, and again, and again.
I believe in the possibility of peace,
    and that peace is a blessing to the world.
I believe that the cross is God's nonviolent embrace of humanity,
    and that all human violence finds its end at the cross of Christ.
I believe that speaking in tongues is a gift of the Spirit;
    freeing our minds from the trammels of rational thought
    to commune with God's Spirit in ways too deep for words.
I believe the Bible offers a revelation of God's truth,
    and that it does so through a series of thought experiments
    concerning the existence of humanity before God.
I believe in marriage as an expression of loving, faithful, equal,
    covenant commitment, between two people, for the blessing of all.
I believe that the earth is a gift,
    and that we have a responsibility before God to tend it care-fully.
I believe that wherever the new humanity in Christ are present,
    the old humanity under death is challenged,
and people are offered transformation to life in all its fullness.

In heaven's name, and for goodness' sake, so help me God, I do believe.

'Broken'

A short story for Good Friday.

Are you sitting comfortably? Good, then I shall begin.

Today I want to tell a story, and it's a story that is both the oldest story that there is, but also, perhaps, the most recent.

It begins in a garden, as ancient stories often do.

This time, it's a garden square on a spring morning in late March. The frosts of winter have finally surrendered, and the early snowdrops and crocuses are offering hope that life yet lies latent in the dead ground.

There's a woman there, eyes closed, warming her face in the morning sun. Her friend, the man, is sitting by her side, reading something and waiting for nothing in particular.

It's one of those days when nothing much happens, but everything seems significant. A perfect moment, of tranquil friendship and quiet hope.

The man lifts his eyes from the page to look at the woman, and she flicks her eyes open to return his gaze.

As their eyes meet, a shadow flashes between them. Maybe it was nothing more than a cloud passing the sun; maybe it was something more. A moment of desire, perhaps; a hint that friendship might turn to something more than companionship.

The woman looks away, and the man looks down, but in that brief second of wordless encounter, something has changed. Tension has entered the garden.

The man mutters silently to himself, remembering a mantra from his childhood, "I want, I want, doesn't get." The woman is more cautious, remembering the last time desire took her by surprise, and she too recites a proverb of caution, reminding herself ruefully that, "one bitten, twice shy."

And so they sit there in silence for a while longer, the woman closing her eyes against the brightness of the sun, the man distracting himself with the words on the page in front of him. But the silence has been broken, and that which is broken is not so easily repaired.

...

Three years later, the silence was broken again, by the wedding bells of a parish church; an appeal to hope, as bride and groom walk each other down the aisle. Friendship surprised by desire had blossomed to something approximating to love, and promises were made in the hope of a better future.

The day had dawned sunny, as weddings days surely should, but by the time of forced smiles for photographs a cloud had started to cast its long shadow.

And it wasn't long before the game we call blame began. "She started it", said the man. "But he deserved it", replied the woman.

Their conversations followed well-worn paths, as the man and the woman discovered the true nature of their deep need of the other. "I love you" became "I need you". A need to be needed, certainly; a need to be loved, sometimes; but more than these, a need to have someone with whom to share the blame of life, the shame, the guilt.

And she became jealous, in time, of the time he gave to the voices on the pages that he read. And he resented her ability to close her eyes and turn her face towards the sun. And each learned to blame the other, for that which had once been so desired.

...

Three years later the silence was broken once again, this time by a baby's cry, as fractured love gave birth to startling innocence; and for a while the frosts of winter melted in the warmth of the hopeful new life that had come into their lives.

A child can, for a while, paper over the cracks in a marriage. And two sons, a few years apart, can offer welcome respite from the lonely tension of two.

The man and the woman discovered a surprising unity of purpose, as they learned together a new game of blame focused not on each other, but on their boys. "Life was so easy until you came along", she said. "Your mother and I have made such sacrifices for you", he echoed.

And so, as they say, the sins of the parents were visited upon the children, and two brothers took the quest for self-justification deep within their young souls. Each brother yearned for acceptance, and each learned who to blame when it was withheld.

Childhood squabbles bred habits of hatred and jealousy, as brother turned against brother.

The elder, for a few brief idyllic years the sole object of his parents' attentions, always resented the imposition his younger brother had made on his memories of those early golden years. "My life was perfect," he would say, "until you came along and ruined everything."

The younger, of course, had no such memories to draw on, he just saw his elder brother getting to everything in life ahead of him. He was, definitionally, years behind, with no way of catching up. He would always be the second son, the perennial prodigal, and it was his destiny in life to be denied the privileges of the firstborn.

In time the brothers grew apart. Separate lives, separate careers, separate families. Occasionally, seasonally, they would meet up with their father, now alone and living an uneasy long silence. The boys would tell him of their lives, hoping for affirmation, but they were always a disappointment.

Until, one Christmas, the younger son announced that he was changing career, following in his father's footsteps. And, for the first time, his father smiled with pride. His son was doing what he had done. He was vindicated.

The father turned accusing eyes on his disappointment of an elder son, who flushed with shame and anger. Meanwhile the younger brother turned to his elder brother in triumph, knowing that for the first and only time in his life he had got there first.

...

FAITH IN DOUBT

The silence of the garden of remembrance was broken by the tears of a woman. A mother crying for her younger son, refusing to be comforted by the man who stood by her side. A couple reunited in grief and guilt. Both sons lost to them, neither one now the keeper of the other, while the blood of the slain cried out from the ground for vindication.

...

And so the story continues, from one garden to another.

...

This time the silence is broken by the sound of a man crying. A man alone with his tears, seeking some release from the burden of shame, and guilt, and grief that has been handed to him. A man longing to pass his suffering on to another, but unable, or unwilling, to do so.

Then there are more men, and some women, and one man betrays his brother with a kiss of death.

The betrayer has realised the futility of projecting hopes and dreams onto another, and so he projects shame and guilt instead.

And then the voices of others join the voice of the first accuser, and guilt is proclaimed over and over and over again, until the brother is guilty enough to deserve the death that is no longer his to refuse.

...

Another garden, a place of death. Women weeping.

Death of love, death of hope, death of fear, death of guilt, death of shame, death of death.

Silence. A shadow. Darkness.

…

Another garden. Silent as the grave.

…

And again, and again, and again, the innocent die to satisfy the guilt of others.

It is both an old story, and a new story. It is our story.

How will it ever end?

That, as they say, is a story for another day…

Imago Dei

One morning, God was staring at the wall.
    Not a blank wall, but not patterned either.
It was a wall of chaos:
    bright colours, dark colours, swirling patterns,
    eternally dark and infinitely bright both at the same time.

God wondered what could be made of the wall,
    and reached out a hand to swirl the colours around.
Soon order and pattern began to emerge:
    luscious pastoral greens coalesced, deep aqua blues combined,
    and this new creation seemed very pleasing to God.

After contemplating the wall for a while longer,
    God began to wonder what to do next,
    so God spoke gently to the wall,
        and a lustrous sheen began to appear.
The wall became shiny, as if a layer of glass had been laid over the top of it.

As God continued to stare at the wall,
    they could now see their own reflection within it.
They saw their image inside their creation.

When they moved their hand,
    the image of God waved back.
When God smiled,
    the image smiled back.
When God blew at the wall,
    the image blew a kiss back.
God loved the image in the wall,
    and was happy with all that that had been made.

But then something unexpected happened.

The image of God reached out and punched the wall from the inside,
    and the shiny surface of the wall now had a flaw in it,
    like a stone-chip on a car windscreen.

Suddenly the image of God didn't look quite so much like God anymore:
    the flaw in the surface had damaged the reflection.

FAITH IN DOUBT

The order that God had brought to the wall was distorted,
       and God was very sad.

But still God stood there, staring at the wall and not turning away.

Then the image hit the wall again,
       this time harder and angrier, as if trying to get out,
       trying to get at God.

God flinched, but still God stared at the wall.

The surface was by now crazed with cracks,
       and the image continued to fragment
       into lots of tiny, sharp fragments.

God contemplated walking away from the wall,
       but knew that to do so would cause the image
       to vanish from the wall forever.

Distorted as it was, it was still her image;
       it was still the image he had loved, waved at, and blown kisses to.

God wondered what to do next.
       And then had an idea.

God took a few steps back, and threw herself violently at the wall.

The force of the impact stunned him and shook the wall,
       and the millions of tiny sharp fragments ripped at their skin.

Powered forward by the momentum of the run-up,
       God seemed for a moment to merge into the wall.

Blood streaked the surface,
       and the mark of the impact was clear to see.

But God had vanished.

FAITH IN DOUBT

After a while it was just possible to make out the faint image of God
    through the crazed, blood-stained, fragmented surface.

God had gone into the wall.

Gradually the image of God grew stronger and larger,
    as God walked up to the wall from the inside.

God reached out a hand and carefully joined two broken shards together,
    and then two more, and then two more.

Gradually, slowly, God began to repair the wall from within.

As God repaired the wall, they looked at it very carefully,
    and started to see their own image reflected back.

The end.

Printed in Great Britain
by Amazon